Mathematics 3
for Young Catholics

by the Seton Staff

Seton Press
Front Royal, Virginia

Executive Editor: Dr. Mary Kay Clark
Editors: Seton Staff

Seton Home Study School
1350 Progress Drive
Front Royal, VA 22630
540-636-9990
540-636-1602 fax

For more information, visit us on the Web at www.setonhome.org.
Contact us by e-mail at counselors@setonhome.org.

ISBN: 978-1-60704-108-5

Cover: *Madonna and Child* by Champaigne

Dedicated to the
Sacred Heart of Jesus

Contents

Introduction

Many of the problems facing our nation today need to be solved by people who develop logical thinking skills as well as excellent mathematical skills. These skills must start in the early grades of schooling. The writer of the Seton elementary math books is a former school teacher and a home schooling teacher of his own several children. He and the Seton staff are dedicated to helping our students solve the issues of our nation so that we can continue to live in a country with liberty and freedom, especially religious freedom.

Students should be shown as often as possible that their math skills are important and useful to them. Parents should think of ways to encourage their children to use their math facts as situations arise around the house as well as in the stores.

Memorizing is imperative, as many math teachers have proclaimed over the years. Your student should be able to give an immediate response to addition and subtraction problems. Understanding is essential as a first step, then repetition, then more patient repetitive practice, until the goal of immediate response can be met.

While no page in this text-workbook should be skipped, once a student has learned a concept and can give an automatic response, some items on a page could be skipped. For students who should have additional practice, we recommend extra drill work. Drill pages and drill workbooks are available on the internet and through Seton.

Be sure that your student has mastered the old before going forward with the new. In a home schooling situation, there is no deadline, no need to push ahead before conquering previous lessons.

We encourage reviewing at least some of the past lessons each day before going on to a new lesson. Don't hesitate to give some math drills, even if only for a couple of minutes. Be sure to give oral drills. At this age when some students are slow in their handwriting, memorizing math facts can be done quickly, and solidifies the math facts in the brain.

Remember this: Mastery can be had only by constant repetition.

Addition Facts Through 10

Mother and the children walk from home to daily Mass for 3 blocks down Chestnut Street and then 2 blocks up Main Street to St. John's Church.

How many blocks do they walk to Mass?

We are looking for the total number of blocks they walk to Mass.

They walk __3__ blocks on Chestnut Street.

They then walk __2__ blocks on Main Street.

To get the total, we add __3__ and __2__ .

__3__ + __2__ = __5__   or
addend addend sum

$$\begin{array}{r} 3 \\ + 2 \\ \hline 5 \end{array}$$ addend
addend
sum

They walk __5__ blocks to Mass.

Exercises

Complete each number sentence.

1. 2 + 7 = __9__
2. 4 + 5 = __9__
3. 3 + 2 = __5__
4. 7 + 3 = __10__

5. 3 + 5 = __8__
6. 4 + 4 = __8__
7. 2 + 2 = __4__
8. 6 + 4 = __10__

Find each sum.

9. $\begin{array}{r} 2 \\ +2 \\ \hline 4 \end{array}$
10. $\begin{array}{r} 6 \\ +4 \\ \hline 10 \end{array}$
11. $\begin{array}{r} 3 \\ +3 \\ \hline 6 \end{array}$
12. $\begin{array}{r} 1 \\ +1 \\ \hline 2 \end{array}$
13. $\begin{array}{r} 6 \\ +0 \\ \hline 6 \end{array}$
14. $\begin{array}{r} 0 \\ +0 \\ \hline 0 \end{array}$

15. $\begin{array}{r} 6 \\ +2 \\ \hline 9 \end{array}$
16. $\begin{array}{r} 2 \\ +3 \\ \hline 5 \end{array}$
17. $\begin{array}{r} 8 \\ +1 \\ \hline 9 \end{array}$
18. $\begin{array}{r} 7 \\ +3 \\ \hline 10 \end{array}$
19. $\begin{array}{r} 4 \\ +5 \\ \hline 9 \end{array}$
20. $\begin{array}{r} 4 \\ +2 \\ \hline 6 \end{array}$

1

Addition Facts Through 10

Practice

Complete each number sentence.

1. 0 + 2 = 2
2. 4 + 3 = 7
3. 7 + 2 = 9

4. 1 + 2 = 3
5. 3 + 6 = 9
6. 8 + 2 = 10

7. 4 + 6 = 10
8. 3 + 3 = 6
9. 0 + 0 = 0

10. 5 + 1 = 6
11. 3 + 5 = 8
12. 3 + 4 = 7

More Practice

Find each sum.

13.
$$\begin{array}{r} 3 \\ +2 \\ \hline 5 \end{array}$$

14.
$$\begin{array}{r} 9 \\ +1 \\ \hline 10 \end{array}$$

15.
$$\begin{array}{r} 0 \\ +6 \\ \hline 6 \end{array}$$

16.
$$\begin{array}{r} 3 \\ +4 \\ \hline 7 \end{array}$$

17.
$$\begin{array}{r} 7 \\ +0 \\ \hline 7 \end{array}$$

18.
$$\begin{array}{r} 1 \\ +4 \\ \hline 5 \end{array}$$

19.
$$\begin{array}{r} 0 \\ +3 \\ \hline 3 \end{array}$$

20.
$$\begin{array}{r} 6 \\ +3 \\ \hline 9 \end{array}$$

21.
$$\begin{array}{r} 2 \\ +2 \\ \hline 4 \end{array}$$

22.
$$\begin{array}{r} 4 \\ +0 \\ \hline 4 \end{array}$$

23.
$$\begin{array}{r} 2 \\ +7 \\ \hline 9 \end{array}$$

24.
$$\begin{array}{r} 4 \\ +4 \\ \hline 8 \end{array}$$

25.
$$\begin{array}{r} 2 \\ +1 \\ \hline 3 \end{array}$$

26.
$$\begin{array}{r} 7 \\ +3 \\ \hline 10 \end{array}$$

27.
$$\begin{array}{r} 0 \\ +7 \\ \hline 7 \end{array}$$

28.
$$\begin{array}{r} 1 \\ +7 \\ \hline 8 \end{array}$$

29.
$$\begin{array}{r} 8 \\ +1 \\ \hline 9 \end{array}$$

30.
$$\begin{array}{r} 1 \\ +6 \\ \hline 7 \end{array}$$

31.
$$\begin{array}{r} 0 \\ +8 \\ \hline 8 \end{array}$$

32.
$$\begin{array}{r} 5 \\ +3 \\ \hline 8 \end{array}$$

33.
$$\begin{array}{r} 3 \\ +7 \\ \hline 10 \end{array}$$

34.
$$\begin{array}{r} 5 \\ +5 \\ \hline 10 \end{array}$$

35.
$$\begin{array}{r} 1 \\ +3 \\ \hline 4 \end{array}$$

36.
$$\begin{array}{r} 0 \\ +0 \\ \hline 0 \end{array}$$

Apply

37. Rosalia found three pennies while sweeping the kitchen. She found six more under the cushion. How many did she find in all?

She found 9 pennies. (9¢)

38. After going to confession, Mary had to say 4 Hail Marys and 5 Our Fathers for penance. How many prayers was she asked to say altogether?

She said 9 prayers in all.

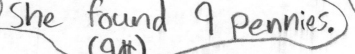

Addition Facts Through 18

John plays on the Seton basketball team. In the last game he scored 8 points in the first half and 7 points in the second half.

How many points did John score in the game?

We are looking for the total number of points John scored in the game.

He scored __8__ points in the first half.

He scored __7__ points in the second half.

To get the total, we add __8__ and __7__.

__8__ + __7__ = __15__   or

$$\begin{array}{r} \boxed{8} \quad \textbf{addend} \\ + \boxed{7} \quad \textbf{addend} \\ \hline \boxed{15} \quad \textbf{sum} \end{array}$$

__8__ + __7__ = __15__
addend   addend   sum

John scored __15__ points in the game.

Exercises

Complete each number sentence.

1. 6 + 8 = __14__   2. 9 + 8 = __17__   3. 4 + 7 = __11__   4. 8 + 8 = __16__

5. 7 + 5 = __12__   6. 6 + 7 = __13__   7. 4 + 8 = __12__   8. 7 + 8 = __15__

Find each sum.

9. $\begin{array}{r} 9 \\ + 4 \\ \hline 13 \end{array}$
10. $\begin{array}{r} 3 \\ + 8 \\ \hline 11 \end{array}$
11. $\begin{array}{r} 7 \\ + 8 \\ \hline 15 \end{array}$
12. $\begin{array}{r} 9 \\ + 9 \\ \hline 18 \end{array}$
13. $\begin{array}{r} 8 \\ + 4 \\ \hline 12 \end{array}$
14. $\begin{array}{r} 9 \\ + 6 \\ \hline 15 \end{array}$

15. $\begin{array}{r} 9 \\ + 3 \\ \hline 12 \end{array}$
16. $\begin{array}{r} 7 \\ + 6 \\ \hline 13 \end{array}$
17. $\begin{array}{r} 7 \\ + 4 \\ \hline 11 \end{array}$
18. $\begin{array}{r} 8 \\ + 6 \\ \hline 14 \end{array}$
19. $\begin{array}{r} 6 \\ + 5 \\ \hline 11 \end{array}$
20. $\begin{array}{r} 9 \\ + 7 \\ \hline 16 \end{array}$

Addition Facts Through 18

Practice

Complete each number sentence.

1. 6 + 7 = 13   2. 8 + 4 = 12   3. 8 + 6 = 14

4. 5 + 9 = 14   5. 7 + 6 = 13   6. 4 + 9 = 13

7. 7 + 4 = 11   8. 7 + 8 = 15   9. 4 + 6 = 10

10. 9 + 9 = 18   11. 7 + 9 = 16   12. 5 + 5 = 10

More Practice

Find each sum.

13. $\begin{array}{r} 4 \\ + 7 \\ \hline 11 \end{array}$ 14. $\begin{array}{r} 5 \\ + 6 \\ \hline 11 \end{array}$ 15. $\begin{array}{r} 9 \\ + 7 \\ \hline 16 \end{array}$ 16. $\begin{array}{r} 8 \\ + 3 \\ \hline 11 \end{array}$ 17. $\begin{array}{r} 9 \\ + 7 \\ \hline 16 \end{array}$ 18. $\begin{array}{r} 7 \\ + 7 \\ \hline 14 \end{array}$

19. $\begin{array}{r} 6 \\ + 8 \\ \hline 14 \end{array}$ 20. $\begin{array}{r} 6 \\ + 6 \\ \hline 12 \end{array}$ 21. $\begin{array}{r} 7 \\ + 5 \\ \hline 12 \end{array}$ 22. $\begin{array}{r} 9 \\ + 4 \\ \hline 13 \end{array}$ 23. $\begin{array}{r} 9 \\ + 3 \\ \hline 12 \end{array}$ 24. $\begin{array}{r} 8 \\ + 4 \\ \hline 12 \end{array}$

25. $\begin{array}{r} 7 \\ + 8 \\ \hline 15 \end{array}$ 26. $\begin{array}{r} 9 \\ + 5 \\ \hline 14 \end{array}$ 27. $\begin{array}{r} 9 \\ + 9 \\ \hline 18 \end{array}$ 28. $\begin{array}{r} 7 \\ + 6 \\ \hline 15 \end{array}$ 29. $\begin{array}{r} 7 \\ + 4 \\ \hline 11 \end{array}$ 30. $\begin{array}{r} 9 \\ + 8 \\ \hline 17 \end{array}$

31. $\begin{array}{r} 8 \\ + 6 \\ \hline 14 \end{array}$ 32. $\begin{array}{r} 6 \\ + 5 \\ \hline 11 \end{array}$ 33. $\begin{array}{r} 8 \\ + 7 \\ \hline 15 \end{array}$ 34. $\begin{array}{r} 7 \\ + 9 \\ \hline 16 \end{array}$ 35. $\begin{array}{r} 8 \\ + 5 \\ \hline 13 \end{array}$ 36. $\begin{array}{r} 5 \\ + 9 \\ \hline 14 \end{array}$

Apply

37. Bernadette and Susan each read six books. How many books is that altogether?

They read 12 books in all.

38. The Seton baseball team scored 7 runs in their last game. Their opponent scored 9 runs. What was the total number of runs scored in the game?

The total number of runs is 16.

4

Subtraction Facts Through 10

Margaret was saying a decade of the Rosary. She was interrupted after her fourth Hail Mary.

How many does she have left to complete the decade?

We need to find the number of Hail Marys she has left to complete the decade.

A decade of the Rosary is _10_ Hail Marys

She prayed _4_ Hail Marys before the interruption.

To get the number left to say, we subtract _4_ from _10_ .

_____ – _____ = _____ or
minuend subtrahend difference

```
   10   minuend
 –  4   subtrahend
 _____
    6   difference
```

Margaret has _6_ Hail Marys left to complete the decade.

Exercises

Complete each number sentence.

1. 8 – 2 = _6_   2. 4 – 2 = _2_   3. 10 – 3 = _7_   4. 9 – 7 = _2_

5. 6 – 2 = _4_   6. 8 – 1 = _7_   7. 7 – 5 = _2_   8. 10 – 8 = _2_

Find each difference.

9.
$$\begin{array}{r} 9 \\ -4 \\ \hline 5 \end{array}$$

10.
$$\begin{array}{r} 6 \\ -3 \\ \hline 3 \end{array}$$

11.
$$\begin{array}{r} 8 \\ -3 \\ \hline 5 \end{array}$$

12.
$$\begin{array}{r} 8 \\ -7 \\ \hline 1 \end{array}$$

13.
$$\begin{array}{r} 6 \\ -2 \\ \hline 4 \end{array}$$

14.
$$\begin{array}{r} 4 \\ -3 \\ \hline 1 \end{array}$$

15.
$$\begin{array}{r} 10 \\ -5 \\ \hline 5 \end{array}$$

16.
$$\begin{array}{r} 6 \\ -4 \\ \hline 2 \end{array}$$

17.
$$\begin{array}{r} 9 \\ -5 \\ \hline 4 \end{array}$$

18.
$$\begin{array}{r} 7 \\ -2 \\ \hline 5 \end{array}$$

19.
$$\begin{array}{r} 10 \\ -9 \\ \hline 1 \end{array}$$

20.
$$\begin{array}{r} 8 \\ -5 \\ \hline 3 \end{array}$$

Practice

Complete each number sentence.

1. 5 − 5 = 0   2. 7 − 3 = 4   3. 1 − 0 = 1

4. 2 − 2 = 0   5. 5 − 1 = 4   6. 6 − 0 = 6

7. 6 − 3 = 3   8. 4 − 3 = 1   9. 7 − 4 = 3

10. 10 − 5 = 5   11. 0 − 0 = 0   12. 5 − 2 = 3

More Practice

Find each difference.

13. $\begin{array}{r} 10 \\ -\ 6 \\ \hline 4 \end{array}$
14. $\begin{array}{r} 4 \\ -\ 2 \\ \hline 2 \end{array}$
15. $\begin{array}{r} 6 \\ -\ 1 \\ \hline 5 \end{array}$
16. $\begin{array}{r} 5 \\ -\ 4 \\ \hline 1 \end{array}$
17. $\begin{array}{r} 7 \\ -\ 6 \\ \hline 1 \end{array}$
18. $\begin{array}{r} 5 \\ -\ 2 \\ \hline 3 \end{array}$

19. $\begin{array}{r} 10 \\ -\ 2 \\ \hline 8 \end{array}$
20. $\begin{array}{r} 9 \\ -\ 4 \\ \hline 5 \end{array}$
21. $\begin{array}{r} 8 \\ -\ 4 \\ \hline 4 \end{array}$
22. $\begin{array}{r} 5 \\ -\ 5 \\ \hline 0 \end{array}$
23. $\begin{array}{r} 7 \\ -\ 5 \\ \hline 2 \end{array}$
24. $\begin{array}{r} 4 \\ -\ 3 \\ \hline 1 \end{array}$

25. $\begin{array}{r} 10 \\ -\ 1 \\ \hline 9 \end{array}$
26. $\begin{array}{r} 7 \\ -\ 1 \\ \hline 6 \end{array}$
27. $\begin{array}{r} 10 \\ -\ 3 \\ \hline 7 \end{array}$
28. $\begin{array}{r} 4 \\ -\ 4 \\ \hline 0 \end{array}$
29. $\begin{array}{r} 5 \\ -\ 3 \\ \hline 2 \end{array}$
30. $\begin{array}{r} 3 \\ -\ 3 \\ \hline 0 \end{array}$

31. $\begin{array}{r} 6 \\ -\ 3 \\ \hline 3 \end{array}$
32. $\begin{array}{r} 9 \\ -\ 2 \\ \hline 7 \end{array}$
33. $\begin{array}{r} 9 \\ -\ 0 \\ \hline 9 \end{array}$
34. $\begin{array}{r} 2 \\ -\ 0 \\ \hline 2 \end{array}$
35. $\begin{array}{r} 9 \\ -\ 8 \\ \hline 1 \end{array}$
36. $\begin{array}{r} 3 \\ -\ 1 \\ \hline 2 \end{array}$

Apply

37. Bernadette checked out 9 books from the library. She read 3 and returned them. How many does she have left to read?

She has 3 more books left to read.

38. Michael scored 8 points in the game. David scored 3 points. How many more points did Michael score in the game than David?

Michael scored 5 more Points than David.

Subtraction Facts Through 18

Ken and Jim both collect Holy Trader cards. Jim has 14 cards and Ken has 9 cards. How many more cards does Jim have than Ken?

We want to know how many more cards Jim has than Ken.

Jim has __14__ Holy Trader cards.

Ken has __9__ Holy Trader cards.

To find the difference, we subtract __9__ from __14__

$$\underset{\text{minuend}}{14} - \underset{\text{subtrahend}}{9} = \underset{\text{difference}}{5} \quad \text{or}$$

$$\begin{array}{r} \boxed{14} \quad \text{minuend} \\ -\ \boxed{9} \quad \text{subtrahend} \\ \hline \boxed{5} \quad \text{difference} \end{array}$$

Jim has __5__ more cards than Ken.

Exercises

Complete each number sentence.

1. $17 - 8 = \underline{9}$
2. $15 - 9 = \underline{6}$
3. $14 - 5 = \underline{9}$
4. $11 - 7 = \underline{4}$

5. $13 - 4 = \underline{9}$
6. $14 - 6 = \underline{8}$
7. $13 - 5 = \underline{8}$
8. $12 - 5 = \underline{7}$

Find each difference.

9. $\begin{array}{r} 18 \\ -\ 9 \\ \hline 9 \end{array}$
10. $\begin{array}{r} 13 \\ -\ 7 \\ \hline 6 \end{array}$
11. $\begin{array}{r} 17 \\ -\ 9 \\ \hline 8 \end{array}$
12. $\begin{array}{r} 14 \\ -\ 9 \\ \hline 5 \end{array}$
13. $\begin{array}{r} 10 \\ -\ 8 \\ \hline 2 \end{array}$
14. $\begin{array}{r} 16 \\ -\ 7 \\ \hline 9 \end{array}$

15. $\begin{array}{r} 11 \\ -\ 5 \\ \hline 6 \end{array}$
16. $\begin{array}{r} 12 \\ -\ 3 \\ \hline 9 \end{array}$
17. $\begin{array}{r} 13 \\ -\ 8 \\ \hline 5 \end{array}$
18. $\begin{array}{r} 10 \\ -\ 3 \\ \hline 7 \end{array}$
19. $\begin{array}{r} 15 \\ -\ 6 \\ \hline 9 \end{array}$
20. $\begin{array}{r} 14 \\ -\ 8 \\ \hline 6 \end{array}$

Subtraction Facts Through 18

Practice

Complete each number sentence.

1. 14 – 6 = _8_   2. 13 – 5 = _8_   3. 12 – 5 = _7_

4. 14 – 7 = _7_   5. 11 – 4 = _7_   6. 15 – 9 = _6_

7. 12 – 8 = _4_   8. 11 – 9 = _2_   9. 13 – 6 = _8_

10. 15 – 7 = _8_   11. 12 – 3 = _9_   12. 16 – 8 = _8_

More Practice

Find each difference.

13. 15
    – 7
    ___
     8

14. 13
    – 6
    ___
     7

15. 13
    – 7
    ___
     6

16. 10
    – 5
    ___
     5

17. 13
    – 5
    ___
     8

18. 11
    – 7
    ___
     4

19. 18
    – 9
    ___
     9

20. 11
    – 6
    ___
     5

21. 16
    – 9
    ___
     7

22. 12
    – 6
    ___
     6

23. 14
    – 8
    ___
     4

24. 15
    – 8
    ___
     5

25. 17
    – 8
    ___
     9

26. 12
    – 8
    ___
     4

27. 14
    – 6
    ___
     8

28. 16
    – 7
    ___
     9

29. 15
    – 3
    ___
    12

30. 17
    – 9
    ___
     8

31. 11
    – 9
    ___
     2

32. 14
    – 9
    ___
     5

33. 16
    – 8
    ___
     8

34. 10
    – 3
    ___
     7

35. 12
    – 5
    ___
     7

36. 14
    – 7
    ___
     7

Apply

37. David has done 15 chapters in his catechism, while his brother, Michael, has only completed 6. How many more chapters has David done than Michael?

38. Jim ran 16 laps around the field. Ken ran 8 laps. How many more laps did Jim run than Ken?

8

A Word About Objectives

In this book, we want to accomplish certain things.
These things that we want to accomplish are called our
goals and **objectives**.
The main overall **goal** of this course is to
help you **build your skills in basic arithmetic**.

Basic arithmetic has **four operations**.
  They are:

1. addition $+$
2. subtraction $-$
3. multiplication $\times$
4. division $\div$

Basic arithmetic has **four sets or kinds of numbers**.
  The four sets of numbers are:

1. whole numbers 0, 1, 2, 3, 4, 5, 6, 7, 8, 9, . . .

2. fractions $\frac{1}{2}, \frac{1}{3}, \frac{1}{4}, \frac{1}{5}, \frac{1}{6}, \frac{1}{7}, \frac{1}{8}, \frac{1}{9}, \frac{1}{10}, \ldots$

3. mixed numbers $1\frac{1}{2}, 2\frac{1}{3}, 3\frac{1}{4}, 4\frac{1}{5}, 5\frac{1}{6}, 6\frac{1}{7}, 7\frac{1}{8}, 8\frac{1}{9}, 9\frac{1}{10}, \ldots$

4. decimals 1.1, 1.2, 1.3, 1.4, 1.5, 1.6, 1.7, 1.8, 1.9, . . .

We are going to be working mainly on these four $+ \quad - \quad \times \quad \div$
operations on these four sets of numbers.

We will also be exploring some geometry, probability,
measurement, graphing, and statistics.

statistics *geometry* *measurement* *graphing* *probability*

Meanwhile, we are ready for our first objective.

Objective #1

The student will memorize the addition and subtraction facts through 18
and will demonstrate his mastery of the facts by completing Skills Tests for
Objective #1 on pp. 187-189 quickly and accurately.

When you have successfully completed the Skills Tests
you may check them off on your objectives list on page 185.

Objectives

9

Properties of Addition

Now we are going to learn a little bit of algebra.

Don't get scared. It's easy. All algebra is, is a type of math that uses symbols to explore the relationships between numbers and the operations used with them.

We already know about the four operations. The operation of addition has some **properties**. That means that addition has certain qualities or characteristics about it.

We call these things **properties**. A **property** is a quality or characteristic particular to a thing.

The Commutative Property of Addition (Order)

Changing the order of the addends does not change the sum.

We can add in any order.

$$1 + 2 = 3 \quad = \quad 2 + 1 = 3$$

Find the sums.

1. $3 + 9 = \underline{12}$ $9 + 3 = \underline{12}$ 2. $7 + 8 = \underline{15}$ $8 + 7 = \underline{15}$

3.
$$\begin{array}{r} 8 \\ +4 \\ \hline 12 \end{array} \qquad \begin{array}{r} 4 \\ +8 \\ \hline 12 \end{array}$$

4.
$$\begin{array}{r} 7 \\ +6 \\ \hline 13 \end{array} \qquad \begin{array}{r} 6 \\ +7 \\ \hline 13 \end{array}$$

5.
$$\begin{array}{r} 9 \\ +5 \\ \hline 14 \end{array} \qquad \begin{array}{r} 5 \\ +9 \\ \hline 14 \end{array}$$

The Associative Property of Addition (Grouping)

Changing the grouping of the addends does not change the sum.

We can group any two addends.

$$(2 + 3) + 4 = 9 \quad = \quad 2 + (3 + 4) = 9$$
$$5 + 4 = 9 \quad = \quad 2 + 7 = 9$$

Find the sums.

6. $6 + 3 + 4 = \underline{13}$ $6 + 3 + 4 = \underline{13}$ 7. $5 + 3 + 9 = \underline{17}$ $5 + 3 + 9 = \underline{17}$

$\underline{9} + 4 = \underline{13}$ $6 + \underline{7} = \underline{13}$ $\underline{8} + 9 = \underline{17}$ $5 + \underline{12} = \underline{17}$

8.
$$\begin{array}{r} 4 \\ 4 \;\boxed{8} \\ +7 \\ \hline 15 \end{array} \qquad \begin{array}{r} 4 \\ 4 \\ +7 \;\boxed{11} \\ \hline 15 \end{array}$$

9.
$$\begin{array}{r} 5 \\ 3 \;\boxed{8} \\ +6 \\ \hline 14 \end{array} \qquad \begin{array}{r} 5 \\ 3 \;\boxed{9} \\ +6 \\ \hline 14 \end{array}$$

10.
$$\begin{array}{r} 2 \\ 7 \;\boxed{9} \\ +3 \\ \hline 12 \end{array} \qquad \begin{array}{r} 2 \\ 7 \;\boxed{10} \\ +3 \\ \hline 12 \end{array}$$

Commutative Property of Addition	Associative Property of Addition
Changing the order of the addends does not change the sum.	Changing the grouping of the addends does not change the sum.

Challenge

1. Does the Commutative Property apply to subtraction? Show an example.

   _____

2. Does the Associative Property apply to subtraction? Show an example.

   _____

The Identity Property (Zero)

Adding zero does not affect the answer.

Find the sums.

3.
$$\begin{array}{r} 8 \\ +0 \\ \hline 6 \end{array} \quad \begin{array}{r} 0 \\ +8 \\ \hline 8 \end{array}$$

$8 + 0 = \underline{8}$

$0 + 8 = \underline{8}$

Subtracting zero does not affect the answer.

Find the differences.

4.
$$\begin{array}{r} 8 \\ -0 \\ \hline 8 \end{array}$$

$8 - 0 = \underline{8}$

We call zero (0) the **identity element** for addition and subtraction.

Inverse Operations (Opposite)

Inverse operations are opposite operations that undo one another.

Subtraction undoes addition and addition undoes subtraction.

They are opposite operations. This is useful for checking your answers.

Check addition by subtracting.

5.
$$\begin{array}{r} 8 \\ +7 \\ \hline 15 \end{array} \quad \begin{array}{r} 15 \\ -7 \\ \hline 8 \end{array}$$

$8 + 7 = \underline{15}$

$15 - 7 = \underline{8}$

Check subtraction by adding.

6.
$$\begin{array}{r} 13 \\ -7 \\ \hline 6 \end{array} \quad \begin{array}{r} 6 \\ +7 \\ \hline 13 \end{array}$$

$13 - 7 = \underline{6}$

$6 + 7 = \underline{13}$

Do You Know?

7. What property of addition has to do with order? _____

8. What property of addition has to do with grouping? _____

9. What property has to do with zero? _____

10. What do we call an operation that undoes another operation? _____

11

Using Properties

1. What is the inverse operation of addition? _____.

2. What is the inverse operation of subtraction? _____.

3. We can check our addition by _____.

4. We can check our subtraction by _____.

Add. Check your work by subtracting.

5. 4 +7 = 11; 11 − 7 = 4

6. 5 +8 = 13; 13 − 8 = 5

7. 6 +7 = 13; 13 − 7 = 6

8. 9 +4 = 13; 13 − 4 = 9

Subtract. Check your work by adding.

9. 14 −6 = 8; 8 + 6 = 14

10. 12 −7 = 5; 5 + 7 = 12

11. 16 −9 = 7; 7 + 9 = 16

12. 9 −5 = 4; 4 + 5 = 9

Find each sum or difference.

13. 7 − 0 = 7

14. 6 + 0 = 6

15. 5 − 0 = 5

16. 4 + 0 = 4

17. 3 − 0 = 3

18. 9 + 0 = 9

Find each sum by grouping any two addends.

19. 5 4 + 5 = 14

20. 7 1 + 2 = 10

21. 2 8 + 3 = 13

22. 6 3 + 4 = 13

23. 4 4 + 2 = 10

24. 5 3 + 6 = 14

Problem Solving Steps

Use these four steps to find answers to word problems.

Step 1. Read

Step 2. Think

What do I know? What does the problem ask me to find out? What should I do? Plan how to solve the problem.

Step 3. Solve

Follow the plan, write the problem and find the answer.

Step 4. Check

Does my answer make sense? Does it answer the question the problem asks? Check your work.

Problem Solving

Read each word problem.

Decide whether to add or subtract to solve the problem.

Then write the problem and find the answer.

1. There were six horses in the barn. James and John each took one for a ride. How many horses were still in the barn?

2. The Martin family has 5 boys and 3 girls. How many children are in the Martin family?

3. A train has twelve cars. It left four at the station. How many cars does the train have now?

4. The Hibls have 11 children. Two are boys. How many are girls?

5. Matt scored 6 points in his first game, 7 points in his second game, and 4 points in his third game. How many points did he score in the three games?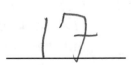

13

6. John studied for 4 hours on Thursday. He also studied 3 hours on Friday, and another 2 hours on Saturday. How many hours did he study altogether?

9

7. *The Letter of Paul to the Romans* has 16 chapters in it. *The Letter of Paul to the Galations* has 6 chapters. How many more chapters did St. Paul write to the Romans than the Galatians?

10

8. *The First Letter of Paul to the Thessalonians* has 5 chapters. *The Second Letter of Paul to the Thessalonians* has 3 chapters. Altogether, how many chapters did St. Paul write to the Thessalonians?

8

9. *The Letter to the Hebrews* has 13 chapters and *The Letter to the Ephesians* has 6 chapters. How many more chapters did the Hebrews receive than the Ephesians?

7

10. *The Letter of James* contains 5 chapters. *The First Letter of Peter* also contains 5 chapters. St. Peter's second letter contains 3 chapters. How many chapters did St. Peter and St. James write altogether?

13

11. *The Book of Tobit* has 14 chapters and *The Book of Amos* has 9. How many more chapters does Tobit have than Amos?

5

12. *The Book of Ruth* has 4 chapters. *The Book of Lamentations* has 5, and *The Book of Baruch* has 6. How many chapters is that altogether?

15

13. *The Second Book of Maccabees* contains 15 chapters. *The Book of Micah* contains 7 chapters. How many more chapters does *2 Maccabees* have than *Micah*?

If you have not already done so, complete the Skills Tests for Objective #1 on pp. 187-189. When you have successfully completed the tests you may check them off on your objectives list on page 185.

14

Multiplication

You can add equal groups
to find the number in all.

You can **multiply** to find how many in all.

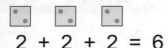

2 + 2 + 2 = 6

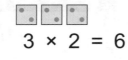

3 × 2 = 6

3 groups of 2

3 × 2

3 times 2

   2 addend
   2 addend
+ 2 addend
  6 sum

   3 factor
× 2 factor
  6 product

multiplication sentence		
factor	factor	product
3 ×	2 =	6
times	equals	

Multiplication

Exercise

Add. Then multiply

1. 3 + 3 + 3 = 9
   3 × 3 = 9

2. 4 + 4 = 8
   2 × 4 = 8

3. 5 + 5 = 10
   2 × 5 = 10

4. 4 + 4 + 4 + 4 = 16
   4 × 4 = 16

5. 5 + 5 + 5 = 15
   3 × 5 = 15

6. 4 + 4 + 4 = 12
   3 × 4 = 12

7. Count by 3s.   0, 3, 6, 9, 12, 15, 18, 21, 24, 27

8. Count by 5s.   0, 5, 10, 15, 20, 25, 30, 35, 40, 45

9. Count by 2s.   0, 2, 4, 6, 8, 10, 12, 14, 16, 18

10. Count by 4s.   0, 4, 8, 12, 16, 20, 24, 28, 32, 36

Look at the multiplication table.

There are 6 **factors** across the top and 6 **factors** down the side.

Let's pick a factor from the side. We will pick the factor 3. Put your finger on the 3.

Now let's pick one from the top. We will pick 5. Put your other finger on the 5.

Now bring your fingers together along the dotted line. In the empty square there, write the product of 3 and 5.

$$3 \times 5 = 15$$

Now let's do it again, only this time pick the 5 from the side and the 3 from the top. Where they meet write the product of 5 and 3.

Are they the same? **Yes!**

$$5 \times 3 = 15$$

Multiplication Table

×	0	1	2	3	4	5
0						
1						
2						
3						
4						
5						

See if you can fill in the rest of the table with the correct products.

Objective #2

The student will memorize the multiplication facts through 81 and will demonstrate his mastery of the facts by completing the Skill Test for Objective #2 on pp. 190-191 quickly and accurately.

When you have successfully completed the Skill Test for Objective #2 you may check it off on your objectives list on page 185.

The Commutative Property of Multiplication (Order)

Changing the order of the factors does not change the product.

We can multiply in any order.

$$3 \times 2 = 6 \quad = \quad 2 \times 3 = 6$$

Find the products.

1. $3 \times 4 = \underline{12}$ $4 \times 3 = \underline{12}$

2. $2 \times 5 = \underline{10}$ $5 \times 2 = \underline{10}$

3.
$$\begin{array}{r} 2 \\ \times 4 \\ \hline 8 \end{array} \qquad \begin{array}{r} 4 \\ \times 2 \\ \hline 8 \end{array}$$

4.
$$\begin{array}{r} 1 \\ \times 5 \\ \hline 5 \end{array} \qquad \begin{array}{r} 5 \\ \times 1 \\ \hline 5 \end{array}$$

5.
$$\begin{array}{r} 3 \\ \times 0 \\ \hline 0 \end{array} \qquad \begin{array}{r} 0 \\ \times 3 \\ \hline 0 \end{array}$$

Multiplication Table

×	0	1	2	3	4	5	6	7	8	9
0										
1										
2										
3										
4										
5										
6										
7										
8										
9										

Learning the Facts

You have a new objective.
The table above lists all the multiplication facts you must learn.

How many factors are listed across the top? <u>10</u>   That's right, 10!

And how many factors are listed down the side? <u>10</u>   That's right, 10 again!

If we have 10 factors and 10 factors, how many products are there in the table? <u>100</u>

You could count all the squares for the number of products or you could multiply:

$$10 \times 10 = 100$$

One hundred products is a lot!
But you can do it! Turn the page
and I'll show you how. See how
many products you can fill in on
this page, by yourself, first.

17

Multiplication Table

×	0	1	2	3	4	5	6	7	8	9
0										
1										
2										
3										
4										
5										
6										
7										
8										
9										

Tip #1

If one of the factors is 0, then the product is 0. That's easy! Fill in all the 0 products. There are 19 products of 0. That only leaves 81 more products to learn.

Tip #2

If one of the factors is 1, then the product is the other factor. That's easy! Fill in all the products with 1 as a factor.

There are 19 products with factors of 1 and 2 of them are already filled in. That only leaves 64 more products to learn.

Tip #3

If you know your addition facts, then you know all the doubles. A double is when 2 is a factor. Fill in all the products with 2 as a factor.

There are 19 products with factors of 2 and 4 of them are already filled in. That only leaves 49 more products to learn.

Fill in as many of the 49 remaining products as you can.

Practice with 0, 1, and 2

Find the products.

1.
$$\begin{array}{r} 3 \\ \times 2 \\ \hline 6 \end{array}$$

2.
$$\begin{array}{r} 9 \\ \times 1 \\ \hline 9 \end{array}$$

3.
$$\begin{array}{r} 0 \\ \times 6 \\ \hline 0 \end{array}$$

4.
$$\begin{array}{r} 5 \\ \times 0 \\ \hline 0 \end{array}$$

5.
$$\begin{array}{r} 3 \\ \times 1 \\ \hline 3 \end{array}$$

6.
$$\begin{array}{r} 7 \\ \times 0 \\ \hline 0 \end{array}$$

7.
$$\begin{array}{r} 1 \\ \times 4 \\ \hline 4 \end{array}$$

8.
$$\begin{array}{r} 2 \\ \times 6 \\ \hline 12 \end{array}$$

9.
$$\begin{array}{r} 2 \\ \times 4 \\ \hline 8 \end{array}$$

10.
$$\begin{array}{r} 8 \\ \times 1 \\ \hline 8 \end{array}$$

11.
$$\begin{array}{r} 1 \\ \times 9 \\ \hline 9 \end{array}$$

12.
$$\begin{array}{r} 0 \\ \times 3 \\ \hline 0 \end{array}$$

13.
$$\begin{array}{r} 2 \\ \times 5 \\ \hline 10 \end{array}$$

14.
$$\begin{array}{r} 0 \\ \times 8 \\ \hline 0 \end{array}$$

×	3	4	5	6	7	8	9
3							
4							
5							
6							
7							
8							
9							

The Squares

If both factors are the same, then we call it a square. Fill in the squares now, if you can. That will leave only 42 products left to learn.

$$3 \times 3 = 9$$

$$4 \times 4 = 16$$

$$5 \times 5 = 25$$

$$6 \times 6 = 36$$

$$7 \times 7 = 49$$

$$8 \times 8 = 64$$

$$9 \times 9 = 81$$

The Commutative Property (Order)

We only have 42 facts left to learn, but the Commutative Property tells us that we can switch the order of the factors, so we really only have 21 more to learn. That's less than the letters in the alphabet! Fill in as many of the remaining products as you can.

Just the Facts, Ma'am

These are your multiplication facts. Please study and learn them all. One helpful way to learn the facts is to copy them down several times.

Objective #2

The student will memorize the multiplication facts through 81 and will demonstrate his mastery of the facts by completing the Skill Test for Objective #2 on pp. 190-191 quickly and accurately.

Zeros	Ones	Twos	Threes	Fours
0 × 0 = 0	1 × 0 = 0	2 × 0 = 0	3 × 0 = 0	4 × 0 = 0
0 × 1 = 0	1 × 1 = 1	2 × 1 = 2	3 × 1 = 3	4 × 1 = 4
0 × 2 = 0	1 × 2 = 2	2 × 2 = 4	3 × 2 = 6	4 × 2 = 8
0 × 3 = 0	1 × 3 = 3	2 × 3 = 6	3 × 3 = 9	4 × 3 = 12
0 × 4 = 0	1 × 4 = 4	2 × 4 = 8	3 × 4 = 12	4 × 4 = 16
0 × 5 = 0	1 × 5 = 5	2 × 5 = 10	3 × 5 = 15	4 × 5 = 20
0 × 6 = 0	1 × 6 = 6	2 × 6 = 12	3 × 6 = 18	4 × 6 = 24
0 × 7 = 0	1 × 7 = 7	2 × 7 = 14	3 × 7 = 21	4 × 7 = 28
0 × 8 = 0	1 × 8 = 8	2 × 8 = 16	3 × 8 = 24	4 × 8 = 32
0 × 9 = 0	1 × 9 = 9	2 × 9 = 18	3 × 9 = 27	4 × 9 = 36

Fives	Sixes	Sevens	Eights	Nines
5 × 0 = 0	6 × 0 = 0	7 × 0 = 0	8 × 0 = 0	9 × 0 = 0
5 × 1 = 5	6 × 1 = 6	7 × 1 = 7	8 × 1 = 8	9 × 1 = 9
5 × 2 = 10	6 × 2 = 12	7 × 2 = 14	8 × 2 = 16	9 × 2 = 18
5 × 3 = 15	6 × 3 = 18	7 × 3 = 21	8 × 3 = 24	9 × 3 = 27
5 × 4 = 20	6 × 4 = 24	7 × 4 = 28	8 × 4 = 32	9 × 4 = 36
5 × 5 = 25	6 × 5 = 30	7 × 5 = 35	8 × 5 = 40	9 × 5 = 45
5 × 6 = 30	6 × 6 = 36	7 × 6 = 42	8 × 6 = 48	9 × 6 = 54
5 × 7 = 35	6 × 7 = 42	7 × 7 = 49	8 × 7 = 56	9 × 7 = 63
5 × 8 = 40	6 × 8 = 48	7 × 8 = 56	8 × 8 = 64	9 × 8 = 72
5 × 9 = 45	6 × 9 = 54	7 × 9 = 63	8 × 9 = 72	9 × 9 = 81

Multiplication Facts

Practice Skip Counting

1. Count by 3s. 0, 3, _6_, _9_, _12_, _15_, _18_, _21_, _24_, _27_

2. Count by 4s. 0, 4, _8_, _12_, _16_, _20_, _24_, _28_, _32_, _36_

3. Count by 5s. 0, 5, _10_, _15_, _20_, _25_, _30_, _35_, _40_, _45_

Practice with 3, 4, and 5

Find the products.

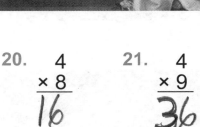

4.
$$\begin{array}{r} 3 \\ \times\ 3 \\ \hline 9 \end{array}$$

5.
$$\begin{array}{r} 3 \\ \times\ 4 \\ \hline 12 \end{array}$$

6.
$$\begin{array}{r} 3 \\ \times\ 5 \\ \hline 15 \end{array}$$

7.
$$\begin{array}{r} 3 \\ \times\ 6 \\ \hline 18 \end{array}$$

8.
$$\begin{array}{r} 4 \\ \times\ 3 \\ \hline 12 \end{array}$$

9.
$$\begin{array}{r} 4 \\ \times\ 4 \\ \hline 16 \end{array}$$

10.
$$\begin{array}{r} 4 \\ \times\ 5 \\ \hline 20 \end{array}$$

11.
$$\begin{array}{r} 4 \\ \times\ 6 \\ \hline 24 \end{array}$$

12.
$$\begin{array}{r} 5 \\ \times\ 3 \\ \hline 15 \end{array}$$

13.
$$\begin{array}{r} 5 \\ \times\ 4 \\ \hline 20 \end{array}$$

14.
$$\begin{array}{r} 5 \\ \times\ 5 \\ \hline 25 \end{array}$$

15.
$$\begin{array}{r} 5 \\ \times\ 6 \\ \hline 30 \end{array}$$

16.
$$\begin{array}{r} 3 \\ \times\ 7 \\ \hline 21 \end{array}$$

17.
$$\begin{array}{r} 3 \\ \times\ 8 \\ \hline 24 \end{array}$$

18.
$$\begin{array}{r} 3 \\ \times\ 9 \\ \hline 27 \end{array}$$

19.
$$\begin{array}{r} 4 \\ \times\ 7 \\ \hline 28 \end{array}$$

20.
$$\begin{array}{r} 4 \\ \times\ 8 \\ \hline 16 \end{array}$$

21.
$$\begin{array}{r} 4 \\ \times\ 9 \\ \hline 36 \end{array}$$

22.
$$\begin{array}{r} 5 \\ \times\ 7 \\ \hline 35 \end{array}$$

23.
$$\begin{array}{r} 5 \\ \times\ 8 \\ \hline 40 \end{array}$$

24.
$$\begin{array}{r} 5 \\ \times\ 9 \\ \hline 45 \end{array}$$

25.
$$\begin{array}{r} 3 \\ \times\ 2 \\ \hline 6 \end{array}$$

26.
$$\begin{array}{r} 4 \\ \times\ 2 \\ \hline 8 \end{array}$$

27.
$$\begin{array}{r} 5 \\ \times\ 2 \\ \hline 10 \end{array}$$

Review

Find the products.

28.
$$\begin{array}{r} 0 \\ \times\ 7 \\ \hline 0 \end{array}$$

29.
$$\begin{array}{r} 1 \\ \times\ 8 \\ \hline 8 \end{array}$$

30.
$$\begin{array}{r} 2 \\ \times\ 9 \\ \hline 18 \end{array}$$

31.
$$\begin{array}{r} 9 \\ \times\ 0 \\ \hline 0 \end{array}$$

32.
$$\begin{array}{r} 8 \\ \times\ 1 \\ \hline 8 \end{array}$$

33.
$$\begin{array}{r} 7 \\ \times\ 2 \\ \hline 14 \end{array}$$

Practice with 3, 4, and 5

Complete each number sentence.

Threes	Fours	Fives
3 × 0 = _____	4 × 0 = _____	5 × 0 = _____
3 × 1 = _____	4 × 1 = _____	5 × 1 = _____
3 × 2 = _____	4 × 2 = _____	5 × 2 = _____
3 × 3 = _____	4 × 3 = _____	5 × 3 = _____
3 × 4 = _____	4 × 4 = _____	5 × 4 = _____
3 × 5 = _____	4 × 5 = _____	5 × 5 = _____
3 × 6 = _____	4 × 6 = _____	5 × 6 = _____
3 × 7 = _____	4 × 7 = _____	5 × 7 = _____
3 × 8 = _____	4 × 8 = _____	5 × 8 = _____
3 × 9 = _____	4 × 9 = _____	5 × 9 = _____

Find the products.

1.   3
   × 6
	2. 3
	   × 8
		3. 3
		   × 7

4.   4
   × 9
	5. 4
	   × 6
		6. 4
		   × 8

7.   5
   × 7
	8. 5
	   × 8
		9. 5
		   × 9

Factors 3, 4, and 5

22

Practice Skip Counting

1. Count by 6s.   0, 6, ____, ____, ____, ____, ____, ____, ____, ____

2. Count by 7s.   0, 7, ____, ____, ____, ____, ____, ____, ____, ____

Practice with 6 and 7

Find the products.

3. $\begin{array}{r} 5 \\ \times 7 \\ \hline \end{array}$
4. $\begin{array}{r} 6 \\ \times 6 \\ \hline \end{array}$
5. $\begin{array}{r} 6 \\ \times 7 \\ \hline \end{array}$
6. $\begin{array}{r} 6 \\ \times 8 \\ \hline \end{array}$

7. $\begin{array}{r} 6 \\ \times 9 \\ \hline \end{array}$
8. $\begin{array}{r} 7 \\ \times 6 \\ \hline \end{array}$
9. $\begin{array}{r} 7 \\ \times 7 \\ \hline \end{array}$
10. $\begin{array}{r} 7 \\ \times 8 \\ \hline \end{array}$

11. $\begin{array}{r} 7 \\ \times 9 \\ \hline \end{array}$
12. $\begin{array}{r} 6 \\ \times 4 \\ \hline \end{array}$
13. $\begin{array}{r} 6 \\ \times 5 \\ \hline \end{array}$
14. $\begin{array}{r} 7 \\ \times 4 \\ \hline \end{array}$

15. $\begin{array}{r} 7 \\ \times 5 \\ \hline \end{array}$
16. $\begin{array}{r} 3 \\ \times 6 \\ \hline \end{array}$
17. $\begin{array}{r} 7 \\ \times 6 \\ \hline \end{array}$
18. $\begin{array}{r} 8 \\ \times 6 \\ \hline \end{array}$
19. $\begin{array}{r} 9 \\ \times 7 \\ \hline \end{array}$
20. $\begin{array}{r} 4 \\ \times 7 \\ \hline \end{array}$

Factors 6 and 7

Fill in the Multiplication Table

×	0	1	2	3	4	5	6	7	8	9
3										
4										
5										
6										
7										

Practice with 6 and 7

Complete each number sentence.

Sixes	Sevens
6 × 0 = _____	7 × 0 = _____
6 × 1 = _____	7 × 1 = _____
6 × 2 = _____	7 × 2 = _____
6 × 3 = _____	7 × 3 = _____
6 × 4 = _____	7 × 4 = _____
6 × 5 = _____	7 × 5 = _____
6 × 6 = _____	7 × 6 = _____
6 × 7 = _____	7 × 7 = _____
6 × 8 = _____	7 × 8 = _____
6 × 9 = _____	7 × 9 = _____

Find the products.

1. 3
   × 6

2. 3
   × 7

3. 7
   × 4

4. 6
   × 4

5. 5
   × 6

6. 5
   × 7

7. 6
   × 1

8. 6
   × 3

9. 6
   × 5

10. 6
   × 7

11. 6
   × 9

12. 6
   × 0

13. 6
   × 2

14. 6
   × 4

15. 6
   × 6

16. 7
   × 7

17. 7
   × 5

18. 7
   × 3

19. 7
   × 1

20. 7
   × 9

21. 7
   × 8

22. 7
   × 6

23. 7
   × 4

24. 7
   × 2

Practice Skip Counting

1. Count by 8s. 0, 8, _____, _____, _____, _____, _____, _____, _____, _____

2. Count by 9s. 0, 9, _____, _____, _____, _____, _____, _____, _____, _____

Practice with 8 and 9

Find the products.

3. 8
    × 6

4. 8
    × 7

5. 8
    × 8

6. 8
    × 9

7. 9
    × 6

8. 9
    × 7

9. 9
    × 8

10. 9
     × 9

11. 8
     × 4

12. 8
     × 5

13. 9
     × 4

14. 9
     × 5

15. 3
     × 8

16. 7
     × 8

17. 8
     × 8

18. 9
     × 9

19. 4
     × 9

20. 5
     × 9

Fill in the Multiplication Table

×	0	1	2	3	4	5	6	7	8	9
5										
6										
7										
8										
9										

Find the products.

1.   3
   × 8

2.   3
   × 9

3.   9
   × 4

4.   8
   × 4

5.   5
   × 8

6.   5
   × 9

Practice with 8 and 9

Complete each number sentence.

Eights	Nines
8 × 0 = _____	9 × 0 = _____
8 × 1 = _____	9 × 1 = _____
8 × 2 = _____	9 × 2 = _____
8 × 3 = _____	9 × 3 = _____
8 × 4 = _____	9 × 4 = _____
8 × 5 = _____	9 × 5 = _____
8 × 6 = _____	9 × 6 = _____
8 × 7 = _____	9 × 7 = _____
8 × 8 = _____	9 × 8 = _____
8 × 9 = _____	9 × 9 = _____

7.   8
   × 1

8.   8
   × 3

9.   8
   × 5

10.   8
   × 7

11.   8
   × 9

12.   8
   × 0

13.   8
   × 2

14.   8
   × 4

15.   8
   × 6

16.   9
   × 7

17.   9
   × 5

18.   9
   × 3

19.   9
   × 1

20.   9
   × 9

21.   9
   × 8

22.   9
   × 6

23.   9
   × 4

24.   9
   × 2

Commutative Property of Multiplication

Changing the order of the factors
does not change the product.

Find the products.

1. 3
    × 6

2. 6
    × 3

3. 7
    × 8

4. 8
    × 7

5. 6
    × 5

6. 5
    × 6

7. 3
    × 7

8. 7
    × 3

9. 8
    × 4

10. 4
     × 8

11. 6
     × 7

12. 7
     × 6

13. 9
     × 3

14. 3
     × 9

15. 8
     × 5

16. 5
     × 8

Identity Property

If one of the factors is one, then
the product is the other factor.

26. $1 \times 5 =$ _____

27. $3 \times 1 =$ _____

28. $1 \times 6 =$ _____

29. $8 \times 1 =$ _____

30. $1 \times 4 =$ _____

Challenge

Find the products.

17. 10
     ×10

18. 11
     ×11

19. 12
     ×12

20. 11
     × 9

21. 11
     ×10

22. 12
     ×10

23. 10
     × 9

24. 11
     × 8

25. 11
     × 7

Zero Property

If one of the factors is zero,
then the product is 0.

31. $0 \times 6 =$ _____

32. $2 \times 0 =$ _____

33. $0 \times 5 =$ _____

34. $0 \times 0 =$ _____

35. $0 \times 7 =$ _____

Problem Solving Steps

Use these four steps to find answers to word problems.

Step 1. Read

Step 2. Think

What do I know? What does the problem ask me to find out?
What should I do? Plan how to solve the problem.

Step 3. Solve

Follow the plan and write the problem and find the answer.

Step 4. Check

Does my answer make sense? Does it answer the question
the problem asks? Check your work.

Problem Solving

Read each word problem.

Decide how to solve the problem.

Then write the problem and find the answer.

1. When Magdalena was learning her times tables,
she practiced for 9 minutes, three times a day.
How many minutes a day did she practice?   _____

2. In a box of chocolates for the Feast of St. Nicholas,
there were 3 rows of chocolates with 8 in each row.
How many chocolates were in the box?   _____

3. If you plant 4 rows of tomatoes, with 7 plants in each row,
how many plants will you have planted, altogether?   _____

4. John studied for 4 hours per day for 4 days.
How many hours of study is that altogether?   _____

5. Matt scored 6 points in each of his three games.
How many points did he score in the three games?   _____

6. There were 5 rows of pennies with 8 pennies in each row.
   How many pennies is that?   _____

7. Peter, James, John, and Andrew went fishing. If each
   caught 3 fish, how many fish did they catch altogether?   _____

8. Father O'Brien bought 8 packages of votive candles
   for St. John's Church this week, and each package
   contained 9 candles. How many new candles does he have?   _____

9. The Seton Crusaders scored two runs in each of the nine
   innings of the baseball game. How many runs did they score? _____

10. Paul is going to read three chapters each day. At the
    end of seven days how many chapters will he have read?   _____

11. The classroom contained 6 rows of desks with 5 desks
    in each row. How many desks were in the classroom?   _____

12. Magdalena did 6 rows of math problems. There were
    6 problems in each row. How many problems did she do?   _____

13. There were 7 bags of marbles in the closet. Each bag
    had 7 marbles in it. How many marbles were there in all?   _____

14. Felicity works for 3 hours a day, 5 days a week.
    How many hours does she work in a week?   _____

15. On a chessboard there are 8 rows of squares with 8 squares
    in each row. How many squares are on a chessboard?   _____

Problem Solving

Add.

1. $\begin{array}{r} 7 \\ +\ 8 \\ \hline \end{array}$
2. $\begin{array}{r} 9 \\ +\ 0 \\ \hline \end{array}$
3. $\begin{array}{r} 6 \\ +\ 9 \\ \hline \end{array}$
4. $\begin{array}{r} 7 \\ +\ 7 \\ \hline \end{array}$
5. $\begin{array}{r} 4 \\ +\ 5 \\ \hline \end{array}$
6. $\begin{array}{r} 6 \\ +\ 4 \\ \hline \end{array}$

7. If John runs four laps and then he runs another three laps, how many laps will he have run?   _____

Subtract.

8. $\begin{array}{r} 15 \\ -\ 8 \\ \hline \end{array}$
9. $\begin{array}{r} 9 \\ -\ 0 \\ \hline \end{array}$
10. $\begin{array}{r} 15 \\ -\ 9 \\ \hline \end{array}$
11. $\begin{array}{r} 16 \\ -\ 8 \\ \hline \end{array}$
12. $\begin{array}{r} 9 \\ -\ 4 \\ \hline \end{array}$
13. $\begin{array}{r} 10 \\ -\ 6 \\ \hline \end{array}$

Review

14. If you plant 13 tomato plants and 7 are killed by frost, then how many tomato plants will you have left?   _____

Multiply.

15. $0 \times 0 =$ _____
16. $2 \times 3 =$ _____
17. $3 \times 0 =$ _____

18. $7 \times 2 =$ _____
19. $8 \times 6 =$ _____
20. $4 \times 4 =$ _____

21. What is the product of seven and three?   _____

22. $\begin{array}{r} 3 \\ \times\ 3 \\ \hline \end{array}$
23. $\begin{array}{r} 0 \\ \times\ 5 \\ \hline \end{array}$
24. $\begin{array}{r} 9 \\ \times\ 0 \\ \hline \end{array}$
25. $\begin{array}{r} 5 \\ \times\ 5 \\ \hline \end{array}$
26. $\begin{array}{r} 1 \\ \times\ 6 \\ \hline \end{array}$
27. $\begin{array}{r} 6 \\ \times\ 6 \\ \hline \end{array}$

28. $\begin{array}{r} 8 \\ \times\ 8 \\ \hline \end{array}$
29. $\begin{array}{r} 4 \\ \times\ 5 \\ \hline \end{array}$
30. $\begin{array}{r} 7 \\ \times\ 6 \\ \hline \end{array}$
31. $\begin{array}{r} 9 \\ \times\ 9 \\ \hline \end{array}$
32. $\begin{array}{r} 7 \\ \times\ 7 \\ \hline \end{array}$
33. $\begin{array}{r} 9 \\ \times\ 8 \\ \hline \end{array}$

If you have not already done so, complete the Skills Test for Objective #2 on pp. 190-191. When you have successfully completed the test you may check it off on your objectives list on page 185.

Division as an Inverse Operation

Division can be thought of in a number of ways.

We can think of division as the inverse operation for multiplication.

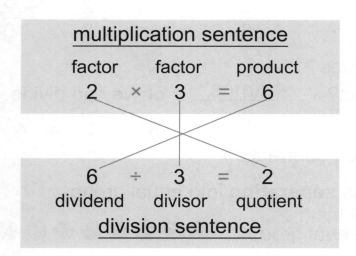

If the product and one factor are known, we can divide the product by the factor and find the other factor.

If   2 × 3 = 6

then 2 = 6 ÷ 3

and 3 = 6 ÷ 2

When we are undoing multiplication with division the **product** is the **dividend**; the known factor is the **divisor** and the unknown factor is the **quotient**.

Inverse Operation Exercise

Write two division sentences for each multiplication sentence. The first one is done for you.

1.   3 × 4 = 12

   12 ÷ 3 = 4

   12 ÷ 4 = 3

2.   4 × 5 = 20

   20 ÷ ___ = ___

   20 ÷ ___ = ___

3.   7 × 3 = 21

   ___ ÷ ___ = ___

   ___ ÷ ___ = ___

4.   2 × 8 = 16

   ___ ÷ ___ = ___

   ___ ÷ ___ = ___

Thinking About Division

How many groups of two are in 8?

We can subtract.

$$
\begin{array}{r} 8 \\ -2 \\ \hline 6 \end{array}
\qquad
\begin{array}{r} 6 \\ -2 \\ \hline 4 \end{array}
\qquad
\begin{array}{r} 4 \\ -2 \\ \hline 2 \end{array}
\qquad
\begin{array}{r} 2 \\ -2 \\ \hline 0 \end{array}
$$

How many times do we subtract? __4 times__ or we can divide.

$$8 \div 2 = 4$$

We can think of division as repeated subtraction.

We can also think about division as **separating** into equal groups.

For example: Separate 8 into 2 equal groups.

How many will be in each group? _____

We can also think about division as **sharing** equally between groups.

For example: Share 8 equally between 2.

How many will each receive? _____

Division as Repeated Subtraction

Exercise

1. How many times can you subtract 3 from 12? _____

2. How many times can you subtract 5 from 15? _____

3. How many times can you subtract 7 from 21? _____

4. 12 ÷ 3 = _____   5. 15 ÷ 5 = _____   6. 21 ÷ 7 = _____

7. Separate 9 into 3 equal groups.
   How many will be in each group?      _____

8. Share 16 equally between 4.
   How many will each receive?      _____

Remember the multiplication table? With the division facts, we start with the products from the multiplication table and we call them dividends.

1	2	3	4	5	6	7	8	9
	4	6	8	10	12	14	16	18
		9	12	15	18	21	24	27
			16	20	24	28	32	36
				25	30	35	40	45
					36	42	48	54
						49	56	63
							64	72
								81

Let's pick a product from the multiplication table and write a division problem with its factors.

Pick a product.   45   I picked 45.

Now list the factors of 45.   9 and 5   Two factors of 45 are 9 and 5.

Now let's write a division problem: $45 \div 9 = 5$

We can also write another division problem: $45 \div 5 = 9$

Try This

Write the factors for each product and then write a division sentence.

Product	Factors		Division Problem
4	2	2	$4 \div 2 = 2$
1. 9	___	___	___ $\div$ ___ = ___
2. 16	___	___	___ $\div$ ___ = ___
3. 25	___	___	___ $\div$ ___ = ___

Write the factors for each product and then write a division sentence.

Product	Factors	Division Problem
1. 36	___ ___	___ ÷ ___ = ___
2. 49	___ ___	___ ÷ ___ = ___
3. 64	___ ___	___ ÷ ___ = ___
4. 81	___ ___	___ ÷ ___ = ___

More About Division

When you divide a number by itself, the quotient is 1.

$$5 ÷ 5 = 1$$

When you divide a number by 1, the quotient is the number.

$$5 ÷ 1 = 5$$

When you divide 0 by a number, the quotient is 0.

$$0 ÷ 5 = 0$$

You CANNOT divide by zero.

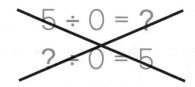

$5 ÷ 0 = ?$
$? ÷ 0 = 5$

Try These

Write the quotients.

5. 12 ÷ 12 = _____   6. 15 ÷ 1 = _____   7. 0 ÷ 7 = _____

8. 10 ÷ 1 = _____   9. 0 ÷ 4 = _____   10. 3 ÷ 3 = _____

11. 0 ÷ 12 = _____   12. 10 ÷ 10 = _____   13. 21 ÷ 1 = _____

Exercise

Write the quotients.

1. 81 ÷ 9 = _____

2. 49 ÷ 7 = _____

3. 25 ÷ 5 = _____

4. 64 ÷ 8 = _____

5. 16 ÷ 4 = _____

6. 9 ÷ 3 = _____

7. 4 ÷ 2 = _____

8. 36 ÷ 6 = _____

9. 1 ÷ 1 = _____

10. 9 ÷ 9 = _____

11. 0 ÷ 9 = _____

12. 7 ÷ 1 = _____

Divide by 2.	**Divide by 3.**	**Divide by 4.**
13. 18 ÷ 2 = _____	22. 27 ÷ 3 = _____	31. 36 ÷ 4 = _____
14. 16 ÷ 2 = _____	23. 24 ÷ 3 = _____	32. 32 ÷ 4 = _____
15. 14 ÷ 2 = _____	24. 21 ÷ 3 = _____	33. 28 ÷ 4 = _____
16. 12 ÷ 2 = _____	25. 18 ÷ 3 = _____	34. 24 ÷ 4 = _____
17. 10 ÷ 2 = _____	26. 15 ÷ 3 = _____	35. 20 ÷ 4 = _____
18. 8 ÷ 2 = _____	27. 12 ÷ 3 = _____	36. 16 ÷ 4 = _____
19. 6 ÷ 2 = _____	28. 9 ÷ 3 = _____	37. 12 ÷ 4 = _____
20. 4 ÷ 2 = _____	29. 6 ÷ 3 = _____	38. 8 ÷ 4 = _____
21. 2 ÷ 2 = _____	30. 3 ÷ 3 = _____	39. 4 ÷ 4 = _____

Division Facts

Exercise

Write the quotients.

1. 27 ÷ 3 = _____   2. 8 ÷ 2 = _____

3. 32 ÷ 4 = _____   4. 15 ÷ 3 = _____

5. 16 ÷ 4 = _____   6. 18 ÷ 2 = _____

7. 12 ÷ 3 = _____   8. 21 ÷ 3 = _____

9. 10 ÷ 2 = _____   10. 28 ÷ 4 = _____

11. 18 ÷ 3 = _____   12. 14 ÷ 2 = _____

Divide by 5.	Divide by 6.	Divide by 7.
13. 45 ÷ 5 = _____	22. 54 ÷ 6 = _____	31. 63 ÷ 7 = _____
14. 40 ÷ 5 = _____	23. 48 ÷ 6 = _____	32. 56 ÷ 7 = _____
15. 35 ÷ 5 = _____	24. 42 ÷ 6 = _____	33. 49 ÷ 7 = _____
16. 30 ÷ 5 = _____	25. 36 ÷ 6 = _____	34. 42 ÷ 7 = _____
17. 25 ÷ 5 = _____	26. 30 ÷ 6 = _____	35. 35 ÷ 7 = _____
18. 20 ÷ 5 = _____	27. 24 ÷ 6 = _____	36. 28 ÷ 7 = _____
19. 15 ÷ 5 = _____	28. 18 ÷ 6 = _____	37. 21 ÷ 7 = _____
20. 10 ÷ 5 = _____	29. 12 ÷ 6 = _____	38. 14 ÷ 7 = _____
21. 5 ÷ 5 = _____	30. 6 ÷ 6 = _____	39. 7 ÷ 7 = _____

Exercise

Divide by 8.

1. 72 ÷ 8 = _____

2. 64 ÷ 8 = _____

3. 56 ÷ 8 = _____

4. 48 ÷ 8 = _____

5. 40 ÷ 8 = _____

6. 32 ÷ 8 = _____

7. 24 ÷ 8 = _____

8. 16 ÷ 8 = _____

9. 8 ÷ 8 = _____

Divide by 9.

10. 81 ÷ 9 = _____

11. 72 ÷ 9 = _____

12. 63 ÷ 9 = _____

13. 54 ÷ 9 = _____

14. 45 ÷ 9 = _____

15. 36 ÷ 9 = _____

16. 27 ÷ 9 = _____

17. 18 ÷ 9 = _____

18. 9 ÷ 9 = _____

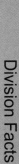

Write the quotients.

19. 35 ÷ 5 = _____

20. 63 ÷ 7 = _____

21. 72 ÷ 8 = _____

22. 28 ÷ 7 = _____

23. 42 ÷ 6 = _____

24. 54 ÷ 9 = _____

25. 27 ÷ 9 = _____

26. 64 ÷ 8 = _____

27. 36 ÷ 6 = _____

28. 24 ÷ 8 = _____

29. 56 ÷ 7 = _____

30. 40 ÷ 5 = _____

31. 36 ÷ 9 = _____

32. 48 ÷ 6 = _____

33. 54 ÷ 6 = _____

34. 48 ÷ 8 = _____

35. 15 ÷ 5 = _____

36. 45 ÷ 9 = _____

Division Facts

37

Another Way to Write Division

Here is another way to write division. The two statements are the same.

$$10 \div 2 = 5 \qquad \text{or} \qquad 2\overline{)10}^{\,5}$$

Try These

Write the quotients.

1. $32 \div 4 =$ _____

2. $4\overline{)16}$

3. $6 \div 2 =$ _____

4. $2\overline{)6}$

5. $16 \div 4 =$ _____

6. $4\overline{)16}$

7. $27 \div 9 =$ _____

8. $9\overline{)27}$

9. $14 \div 7 =$ _____

10. $7\overline{)14}$

11. $81 \div 9 =$ _____

12. $9\overline{)81}$

13. $72 \div 8 =$ _____

14. $8\overline{)72}$

15. $18 \div 9 =$ _____

16. $9\overline{)18}$

17. $7\overline{)35}$

18. $6\overline{)42}$

19. $8\overline{)64}$

20. $6\overline{)54}$

21. $8\overline{)40}$

22. $5\overline{)25}$

23. $9\overline{)36}$

24. $7\overline{)49}$

25. $3\overline{)15}$

26. $5\overline{)30}$

27. $8\overline{)72}$

28. $9\overline{)45}$

29. $7\overline{)56}$

30. $9\overline{)63}$

Objective #3

The student will memorize the division facts through 81 and will demonstrate his mastery of the facts by completing the Skill Test for Objective #3 on pp. 192-193 quickly and accurately.

Division Practice

Practice

Write the quotients.

1. $3\overline{)6}$ 2. $2\overline{)4}$ 3. $3\overline{)21}$

4. $1\overline{)1}$ 5. $1\overline{)2}$ 6. $4\overline{)8}$

7. $6\overline{)18}$ 8. $1\overline{)4}$ 9. $3\overline{)27}$

10. $3\overline{)12}$ 11. $2\overline{)16}$ 12. $4\overline{)16}$ 13. $7\overline{)14}$

14. $3\overline{)6}$ 15. $3\overline{)24}$ 16. $3\overline{)9}$ 17. $4\overline{)12}$

Write the quotients.

18. $12 \div 3 =$ _____   19. $48 \div 8 =$ _____   20. $49 \div 7 =$ _____

21. $27 \div 9 =$ _____   22. $20 \div 4 =$ _____   23. $54 \div 6 =$ _____

24. $28 \div 7 =$ _____   25. $64 \div 8 =$ _____   26. $35 \div 5 =$ _____

27. $25 \div 5 =$ _____   28. $36 \div 6 =$ _____   29. $40 \div 8 =$ _____

30. $27 \div 3 =$ _____   31. $36 \div 4 =$ _____   32. $21 \div 3 =$ _____

33. $16 \div 1 =$ _____   34. $16 \div 2 =$ _____   35. $16 \div 4 =$ _____

Division Practice

We can think of division as the inverse operation for multiplication.

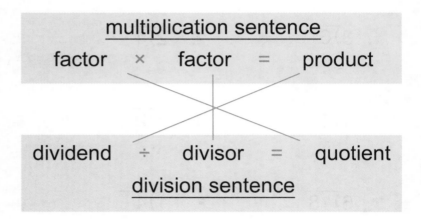

multiplication sentence

factor × factor = product

dividend ÷ divisor = quotient

division sentence

If the product and one factor are known, we can divide the product by the factor and find the other factor.

We can think of division as repeated subtraction.

Another way to think about division is as **separating** into equal groups.

We can also think about division as **sharing** equally between groups

Rules Review

When you divide a number by itself, the quotient is 1.	**When you divide a number by 1, the quotient is the number.**

$$\text{number} \div \text{itself} = 1$$

$$\text{number} \div 1 = \text{number}$$

When you divide 0 by a number, the quotient is 0.	**You CANNOT divide by zero.**

$$0 \div \text{any number} = 0$$

~~any number ÷ 0 = ?~~

If you have not already done so, complete the Skills Tests for Objective #3 on pp. 192-193. When you have successfully completed the test you may check it off on your objectives list on page 185.

Place Value

All numerals can be written with only ten **digits**.

0   1   2   3   4
5   6   7   8   9

It is the place that the **digit** occupies that gives the number its **value**. 53 and 35 are not the same number but they have the same **digits**.

This year we will work with numbers up to six places.
The biggest number we will work with is 999,999.
It has six places and the largest **digit** in each place.
We say it as:

nine hundred ninety-nine thousand nine hundred ninety-nine!

Here is a chart that tells you the names of the six places.
Below it is a chart that shows you the numbers of the six places.

10 ten thousands is 1 hundred thousand

10 thousands is 1 ten thousand

10 hundreds is 1 thousand

10 tens is 1 hundred

10 ones is 1 ten

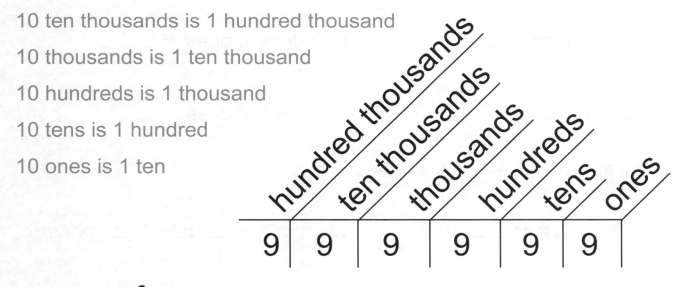

hundred thousands	ten thousands	thousands	hundreds	tens	ones
9	9	9	9	9	9

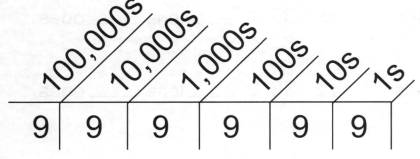

100,000s	10,000s	1,000s	100s	10s	1s
9	9	9	9	9	9

$$100,000 = 10^5$$
$$10,000 = 10^4$$
$$1,000 = 10^3$$
$$100 = 10^2$$
$$10 = 10^1$$
$$1 = 10^0$$

Place Value

The **place** of a **digit** determines its **value**.

5 tens 3 ones = 53

3 tens 5 ones = 35

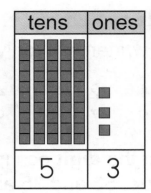
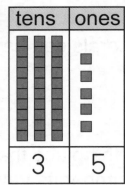

tens	ones	tens	ones
5	3	3	5

Exercise

Write the numbers.

1. 5 tens 9 ones = _____

2. 9 tens 0 ones = _____

3. 3 tens 7 ones = _____

4. 8 tens 4 ones = _____

5. 1 ten 5 ones = _____

6. 4 tens 2 ones = _____

7. 6 tens 3 ones = _____

8. 3 tens 6 ones = _____

9. 7 tens 1 one = _____

10. 2 tens 8 ones = _____

Write the place value for each number.

11. 79 = _____ tens _____ ones

12. 55 = _____ tens _____ ones

13. 26 = _____ tens _____ ones

14. 32 = _____ tens _____ ones

15. 58 = _____ tens _____ ones

16. 83 = _____ tens _____ ones

17. 64 = _____ tens _____ ones

18. 91 = _____ tens _____ ones

Tens and Ones

Hundreds

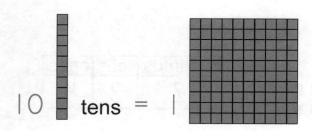

hundreds | tens | ones
1 | 0 | 0

10 tens = 100

10 tens = 1 hundred or 100.

Exercise

Write the numbers.

1. | hundreds | tens | ones |
   | 1 | 2 | 3 |
   _____

2. | hundreds | tens | ones |
   | 5 | 1 | 8 |
   _____

3. | hundreds | tens | ones |
   | 3 | 4 | 5 |
   _____

4. | hundreds | tens | ones |
   | 8 | 3 | 6 |
   _____

5. | hundreds | tens | ones |
   | 5 | 6 | 7 |
   _____

6. | hundreds | tens | ones |
   | 9 | 5 | 4 |
   _____

7. | hundreds | tens | ones |
   | 7 | 8 | 9 |
   _____

8. | hundreds | tens | ones |
   | 6 | 7 | 2 |
   _____

9. | hundreds | tens | ones |
   | 2 | 0 | 0 |
   _____

10. | hundreds | tens | ones |
   | 4 | 9 | 1 |
   _____

Hundreds

43

Hundreds

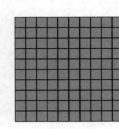 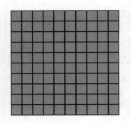 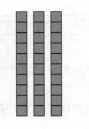

hundreds	tens	ones
2	3	4

234

Standard Form

200 + 30 + 4

Expanded Form

two hundred thirty-four

Word Name

Exercise

Write the number in standard form.

1. 700 + 10 + 3 _____

2. 900 + 80 + 5 _____

3. 300 + 70 + 2 _____

4. 500 + 20 + 8 _____

5. 200 + 30 + 1 _____

6. 800 + 60 + 4 _____

7. 100 + 50 + 9 _____

8. 400 + 40 + 7 _____

Write the number in expanded form.

9. 362 = ____ hundreds ____ tens ____ ones = _____ + _____ + _____

10. 591 = ____ hundreds ____ tens ____ ones = _____ + _____ + _____

11. 743 = ____ hundreds ____ tens ____ ones = _____ + _____ + _____

12. 568 = ____ hundreds ____ tens ____ ones = _____ + _____ + _____

Hundreds

44

13. 453 = ____ hundreds ____ tens ____ ones = _____ + _____ + _____

14. 981 = ____ hundreds ____ tens ____ ones = _____ + _____ + _____

15. 674 = ____ hundreds ____ tens ____ ones = _____ + _____ + _____

16. 865 = ____ hundreds ____ tens ____ ones = _____ + _____ + _____

Keeping in Shape

Add.

1.	2.	3.	4.	5.	6.
7 + 8	9 + 5	6 + 9	7 + 7	4 + 5	6 + 4

Subtract.

7.	8.	9.	10.	11.	12.
15 − 8	9 − 3	15 − 9	16 − 7	9 − 4	10 − 6

Multiply.

13.	14.	15.	16.	17.	18.
3 × 3	0 × 5	7 × 3	5 × 5	2 × 6	6 × 6

Divide.

19. $24 \div 4 =$ _____   20. $4\overline{)32}$ 21. $10 \div 2 =$ _____   22. $2\overline{)6}$

23. $12 \div 4 =$ _____   24. $4\overline{)16}$ 25. $36 \div 9 =$ _____   26. $9\overline{)27}$

27. $21 \div 7 =$ _____   28. $7\overline{)14}$ 29. $72 \div 9 =$ _____   30. $9\overline{)81}$

Thousands

1 thousand = 10 hundreds

Say: one thousand   Write: 1000 or 1,000

Place value: 1 thousand 0 hundreds 0 tens 0 ones

Exercise

Write the numbers.

1.

thousands	hundreds	tens	ones
8	1	6	2

_____

2.

thousands	hundreds	tens	ones
2	8	1	1

_____

3.

thousands	hundreds	tens	ones
6	3	8	4

_____

4.

thousands	hundreds	tens	ones
9	6	3	9

_____

5.

thousands	hundreds	tens	ones
4	5	4	6

_____

6.

thousands	hundreds	tens	ones
7	4	5	0

_____

7.

thousands	hundreds	tens	ones
2	7	2	8

_____

8.

thousands	hundreds	tens	ones
5	2	7	7

_____

9.

thousands	hundreds	tens	ones
1	9	0	3

_____

10.

thousands	hundreds	tens	ones
3	0	9	5

_____

Exercise

Write the place value and the number.

1. five thousand three hundred twenty-three

_____thousands _____hundreds _____tens _____ones _____

2. two thousand five hundred twenty-five

_____thousands _____hundreds _____tens _____ones _____

3. nine thousand seven hundred forty-seven

_____thousands _____hundreds _____tens _____ones _____

4. six thousand nine hundred sixty-eight

_____thousands _____hundreds _____tens _____ones _____

5. three thousand two hundred eighty-six

_____thousands _____hundreds _____tens _____ones _____

6. eight thousand four hundred seventy-four

_____thousands _____hundreds _____tens _____ones _____

7. seven thousand six hundred ninety-two

_____thousands _____hundreds _____tens _____ones _____

Thousands

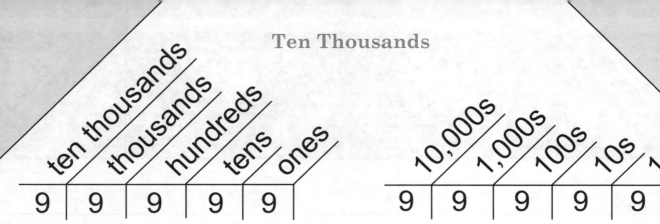

ten thousands	thousands	hundreds	tens	ones
9	9	9	9	9

10,000s	1,000s	100s	10s	1s
9	9	9	9	9

Exercise

Write the numbers.

1.
7	6	3	8	1	_____
ten thousands	thousands	hundreds	tens	ones	

2.
5	9	5	6	3	_____
ten thousands	thousands	hundreds	tens	ones	

3.
9	4	7	4	5	_____
ten thousands	thousands	hundreds	tens	ones	

4.
2	7	9	2	7	_____
ten thousands	thousands	hundreds	tens	ones	

5.
4	3	2	9	2	_____
ten thousands	thousands	hundreds	tens	ones	

6.
8	8	4	7	4	_____
ten thousands	thousands	hundreds	tens	ones	

7.
6	5	6	5	6	_____
ten thousands	thousands	hundreds	tens	ones	

8.
3	2	8	3	8	_____
ten thousands	thousands	hundreds	tens	ones	

Exercise

Write the place value and the number.

1. thirty-one thousand four hundred twenty-one   _____

   _____ _____ _____ _____ _____
   ten thousands thousands hundreds tens ones

2. sixty-four thousand five hundred thirty-five   _____

   _____ _____ _____ _____ _____
   ten thousands thousands hundreds tens ones

3. twenty-seven thousand six hundred nineteen   _____

   _____ _____ _____ _____ _____
   ten thousands thousands hundreds tens ones

4. fifty-two thousand four hundred forty-six   _____

   _____ _____ _____ _____ _____
   ten thousands thousands hundreds tens ones

5. seventy thousand two hundred fifty-nine   _____

   _____ _____ _____ _____ _____
   ten thousands thousands hundreds tens ones

6. forty-five thousand seven hundred twenty-six   _____

   _____ _____ _____ _____ _____
   ten thousands thousands hundreds tens ones

Hundred Thousands

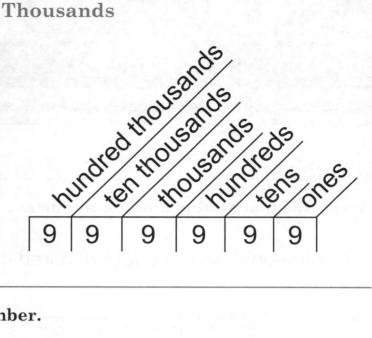

hundred thousands	ten thousands	thousands	hundreds	tens	ones
9	9	9	9	9	9

Exercise

Write the place values for each number.

1. 369,450
    three hundred sixty-nine thousand four hundred fifty

    ___ hundred thousands ___ ten thousands ___ thousands ___ hundreds ___ tens ___ ones

2. 123,456
    one hundred twenty-three thousand four hundred fifty-six

    ___ hundred thousands ___ ten thousands ___ thousands ___ hundreds ___ tens ___ ones

3. 687,291
    six hundred eighty-seven thousand two hundred ninety-one

    ___ hundred thousands ___ ten thousands ___ thousands ___ hundreds ___ tens ___ ones

4. 335,951
    three hundred thirty-five thousand nine hundred fifty-one

    ___ hundred thousands ___ ten thousands ___ thousands ___ hundreds ___ tens ___ ones

5. 717,241

seven hundred seventeen thousand two hundred forty-one

_____ _____ _____ _____ _____ _____
hundred thousands ten thousands thousands hundreds tens ones

6. 249,309

two hundred forty-nine thousand three hundred nine

_____ _____ _____ _____ _____ _____
hundred thousands ten thousands thousands hundreds tens ones

7. 525,750

five hundred twenty-five thousand seven hundred fifty

_____ _____ _____ _____ _____ _____
hundred thousands ten thousands thousands hundreds tens ones

8. 475,300

four hundred seventy-five thousand three hundred

_____ _____ _____ _____ _____ _____
hundred thousands ten thousands thousands hundreds tens ones

9. 596,015

five hundred ninety-six thousand fifteen

_____ _____ _____ _____ _____ _____
hundred thousands ten thousands thousands hundreds tens ones

Hundred Thousands

Standard and Expanded Form

Example: four hundred thirty-one thousand five hundred twenty-six

Standard Form: 431,526

Expanded Form:

400,000 + 30,000 + 1,000 + 500 + 20 + 6

Exercise

Write in standard and expanded form.

1. seven hundred forty-nine thousand six hundred thirty-five

   _____

   _____ + _____ + _____ + _____ + _____ + _____

2. eight hundred eighty-one thousand two hundred forty-two

   _____

   _____ + _____ + _____ + _____ + _____ + _____

3. nine hundred fifty-three thousand seven hundred nineteen

   _____

   _____ + _____ + _____ + _____ + _____ + _____

4. six hundred nine thousand eight hundred sixty-six

   _____

   _____ + _____ + _____ + _____ + _____ + _____

Standard and Expanded Form

5. seven hundred fifteen thousand two hundred fifty-nine

    _____

    _____+_____+_____+_____+_____+_____

6. one hundred forty-five thousand three hundred fifty-six

    _____

    _____+_____+_____+_____+_____+_____

7. four hundred twelve thousand seven hundred seventy-six

    _____

    _____+_____+_____+_____+_____+_____

8. five hundred fifty-seven thousand two hundred seventy-five

    _____

    _____+_____+_____+_____+_____+_____

9. two hundred forty-one thousand nine hundred seven

    _____

    _____+_____+_____+_____+_____+_____

Comparing Numbers

The first thing to check when comparing whole numbers is the number of digits in each number. The number with the most digits is the larger number.

Example: Compare 1,234 and 567

1,234 has four digits and 567 has three digits.

1,234 is greater than 567

If the number of digits is the same, then we start on the left and compare.

Example: Compare 1,234 and 5,678

We see that each number has four digits. We start on the left and compare the digits in the thousands place: 5 is greater than 1.

Then: 5,678 is greater than 1,234

Exercise

Compare each set of numbers and circle the one that is greater.

1.   2,479 and   352

2.   3,229 and   6,917

3.   998 and   8,778

4.   2,616 and   3,254

5.   123 and   78

6.   6,987 and   7,987

7.   97 and   4,312

8.   7,000 and   6,000

9.   359 and   5,613

10.   5,943 and   4,578

11.   7,296 and   962

12.   1,429 and   3,215

Comparing Numbers

Comparing Numbers

If the number of digits is the same
then we start on the left and compare.
Find the first place the digits are different

Example: Compare 3,568 and 3,567

We see that each number has four digits.

We start on the left and compare the digits
in the thousands place: They are the same.

We move to the hundreds place: They are the same.

We move to the tens place: They are the same.

We move to the ones place: 8 is greater than 7.

Then: 3,568 is greater than 3,567

Exercise

Compare each set of numbers and circle the one that is greater.

1. 3,481 and   3,492   2.   798   and   634

3. 4,376 and   4,385   4.   927   and   928

5. 7,789 and   7,698   6.   2,295 and   2,265

7. 8,529 and   8,576   8.   6,396 and   9,663

9. 3,325 and   3,523   10.   5,847 and   6,847

11. 6,840 and   6,825   12.   37,456 and   37,465

13. 5,987 and   5,978   14.   92,987 and   92,978

(Tip: The small end should point to the smaller number.)

Exercise

Compare. Write < or > in the circle.

1. 425 ◯ 1,425

2. 5,967 ◯ 3,125

3. 627 ◯ 217

4. 6,524 ◯ 6,529

5. 4,290 ◯ 8,221

6. 37,489 ◯ 3,748

7. 100 ◯ 266

8. 4,563 ◯ 4,567

9. 642 ◯ 6,942

10. 23,569 ◯ 22,758

11. 1,500 ◯ 629

12. 45,123 ◯ 46,123

13. 844 ◯ 842

14. 392 ◯ 5,847

15. 111 ◯ 121

16. 63,925 ◯ 69,235

17. 596 ◯ 695

18. 4,501 ◯ 4,105

19. 958 ◯ 399

20. 2,564 ◯ 2,645

21. 497 ◯ 1,000

22. 5,000 50,000

greater than – less than

Rounding Numbers

Sometimes you will be asked to **round** a number to a certain place.

For example, you might want to round a number to the nearest **ten**.

Example: Round 43 to the nearest ten.

Ask yourself: What tens is 43 between?

Answer: 43 is between 40 and 50.

Now we round up or round down depending on which is nearer.
Is 43 nearer to 40 or nearer to 50?

43 is nearer to 40 so we round **down** to 40.

43 **rounded** *to the nearest ten* is 40.

Now you try this one: Round 57 to the nearest ten.

What tens is 57 between?   _____ and _____.

Which is nearer?   _____   We round **up**.

57 rounded to the nearest ten is 60.

<u>Try These</u>

Round each to the nearest ten.

1.   32   _____   2.   66   _____

3.   98   _____   4.   369   _____

5.   54   _____   6.   122   _____

7.   196   _____   8.   344   _____

Rounding Numbers

We have learned that we round up or down depending upon which is nearer. What about when it is exactly halfway between?

Halfway or more we round **up**.   **Less than halfway** we round **down**.

Example: Round 45 to the nearest ten.

Ask yourself: What tens is 45 between?

Answer: 45 is between 40 and 50.

45 is halfway between 40 and 50 so we round **up** to 50.

45 **rounded** *to the nearest ten* is 50.

Try These

Round each to the nearest ten.

1. 74 _____

2. 2,485 _____

3. 1,245 _____

4. 98 _____

5. 152 _____

6. 489 _____

7. 28 _____

8. 625 _____

9. 35 _____

10. 48,241 _____

11. 439 _____

12. 89 _____

13. 25 _____

14. 12,823 _____

Rounding Numbers

Rounding to the Nearest Hundred

Rounding to the nearest hundred is just like rounding to the nearest ten. Rounding to the nearest hundred is just one place over.

Instead of between tens, we are between hundreds.

Halfway or more we round **up**.   **Less than halfway** we round **down**.

Example: Round 462 to the nearest hundred.

Ask yourself: What hundreds is 462 between?

Answer: 462 is between 400 and 500.

462 is nearer to 500 so we round **up** to 500.

462 **rounded** *to the nearest hundred* is 500.

Try These

Round each to the nearest hundred.

1.   164   _____   2.   701   _____

3.   6,885   _____   4.   859   _____

5.   2,888   _____   6.   874   _____

7.   348   _____   8.   2,357   _____

9.   541   _____   10.   9,851   _____

11.   665   _____   12.   888   _____

13.   892   _____   14.   7,992   _____

Rounding to the Nearest Thousand

Rounding to the nearest thousand is just like rounding to the nearest hundred. Rounding to the nearest thousand is just one place over from the hundreds place.

Instead of between hundreds we are between thousands.

Halfway or more we round **up**.
Less than halfway we round **down**.

Example: Round 64,582 to the nearest thousand.

Ask yourself: What thousands is 64,582 between?

Answer: 64,582 is between 64,000 and 65,000.

64,582 is nearer to 65,000 so we round **up** to 65,000.

64,582 **rounded** *to the nearest thousand* is 65,000.

Try These

Round each to the nearest thousand.

1.   5,523   _____

2.   4,326   _____

3.   62,479   _____

4.   8,729   _____

5.   43,631   _____

6.   7,833   _____

7.   92,541   _____

8.   66,245   _____

9.   81,892   _____

10.   75,586   _____

11.   53,574   _____

12.   86,542   _____

Rounding to the Nearest Thousand

Rounding Exercise

Round each to the nearest ten.

1. 67,024 _____

2. 427 _____

3. 382 _____

4. 5,493 _____

5. 8,922 _____

6. 555 _____

7. 784 _____

8. 54,928 _____

Round each to the nearest hundred.

9. 2,698 _____

10. 245 _____

11. 376 _____

12. 545 _____

13. 2,456 _____

14. 3,617 _____

15. 922 _____

16. 862 _____

Round each to the nearest thousand.

17. 3,501 _____

18. 91,279 _____

19. 45,632 _____

20. 8,342 _____

21. 6,794 _____

22. 67,590 _____

23. 78,522 _____

24. 54,532 _____

Write in standard and expanded form.

1. six hundred twenty-nine thousand, four hundred fifty-five

_____

_____+_____+_____+_____+_____+_____

2. four hundred seventy-three thousand, six hundred thirty-nine

_____

_____+_____+_____+_____+_____+_____

3. five hundred ninety-three thousand, two hundred fifteen

_____

_____+_____+_____+_____+_____+_____

Compare. Write < or > in the circle.

4. 777 ◯ 888

5. 100 ◯ 1,000

6. 5,450 ◯ 5,540

7. 389 ◯ 401

8. 3,789 ◯ 3,798

9. 7,416 ◯ 7,412

10. 22,525 ◯ 19,728

11. 728 ◯ 637

12. 587,642 ◯ 63,257

13. 540,231 ◯ 541,639

Adding Whole Numbers With More Than One Digit

When adding whole numbers we always start with the ones place.

Add: **24 + 35**

First we rewrite vertically:

Make sure the ones and tens are lined up with one another.

$$\begin{array}{r} 24 \\ +35 \\ \hline \end{array}$$

Start by adding the ones.

Then add the tens.

$$\begin{array}{r} 24 \\ +35 \\ \hline 9 \end{array} \qquad \begin{array}{r} 24 \\ +35 \\ \hline 59 \end{array}$$

Exercise

Add.

1. 42 +30 2. 81 +15 3. 26 +33 4. 34 +34 5. 70 +22

6. 51 +21 7. 22 +47 8. 63 +36 9. 17 +31 10. 20 +61

11. 33 +44 12. 65 +11 13. 26 +53 14. 73 +16 15. 83 +11

Problem Solving

**Read each word problem.
Then write the addition problem and find the answer.**

16. Mr. Kosten planted 47 tomato plants on Monday and 32 on Tuesday. How many plants did he plant? _____

17. There were 23 girls making their First Holy Communion and 25 boys. How many children were making their First Holy Communion? _____

63

Adding 3 and 4-Digit Numbers

No matter how large the numbers are, we always start with the ones place.

Add: 244 + 352

First we rewrite vertically:

$$\begin{array}{r} 244 \\ +352 \\ \hline \end{array}$$

Make sure all the places are lined up with one another.

Then we start with the ones and move left.

Add the ones.	Add the tens	Add the hundreds.
$\begin{array}{r} 244 \\ +352 \\ \hline 6 \end{array}$	$\begin{array}{r} 244 \\ +352 \\ \hline 96 \end{array}$	$\begin{array}{r} 244 \\ +352 \\ \hline 596 \end{array}$

Example: Add: 3246 + 4512

First we rewrite vertically:

$$\begin{array}{r} 3246 \\ +4512 \\ \hline \end{array}$$

Make sure all the places are lined up with one another.

Then we start with the ones and move left.

Add the ones.	Add the tens	Add the hundreds	Add the thousands
$\begin{array}{r} 3246 \\ +4512 \\ \hline 8 \end{array}$	$\begin{array}{r} 3246 \\ +4512 \\ \hline 58 \end{array}$	$\begin{array}{r} 3246 \\ +4512 \\ \hline 758 \end{array}$	$\begin{array}{r} 3246 \\ +4512 \\ \hline 7758 \end{array}$

Now you try: Add: 2134 + 3732

Objective #4 – Addition of Whole Numbers

The student will be able to add whole numbers and multiple addends up to the sum of 999,999 and will demonstrate his mastery by completing the Skill Test for Objective #4 on pp. 194-195 quickly and accurately.

Exercise

Add.

1. 72
   +14

2. 65
   +20

3. 82
   +17

4. 32
   +44

5. 12
   +86

6. 612
   +375

7. 437
   +261

8. 139
   +860

9. 247
   +351

10. 765
    +123

11. 3223
    +5471

12. 6416
    +1542

13. 3521
    +4367

14. 2437
    +5361

15. 6584
    +1212

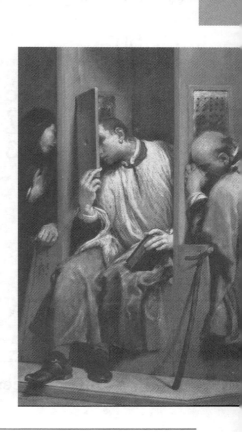

16. 4765
    +3232

17. 2363
    +4521

18. 4561
    +2230

Problem Solving

Read each problem.
Then write the addition problem and find the answer.

19. Seton enrolled 2,450 new students in July
    and 3,239 students in August. How many
    new students were enrolled in July and August?   _____

20. The first day of their trip, the Martin family
    drove 302 miles from Front Royal to New York.
    The second day they drove 215 miles from
    New York to Boston. How many miles did
    they drive altogether from Front Royal to Boston?   _____

Adding Whole Numbers With Regrouping

When adding whole numbers we always start with the ones place.

Add: **56 + 27**

First we rewrite vertically:

$$\begin{array}{r} 56 \\ +27 \\ \hline \end{array}$$

Make sure the ones and tens are lined up with one another.

We start by adding the ones.

$$\begin{array}{r} 56 \\ +27 \\ \hline \end{array}$$

$$\begin{array}{r} 1 \\ 56 \\ +27 \\ \hline 3 \end{array}$$

We notice that 6 + 7 is 13.

How do we write 13 in the ones place?

We can't so we **regroup**.

13 ones is the same as 1 ten and 3 ones.

We put the 1 ten at the top of the tens place and we put the 3 ones in the ones place.

$$\begin{array}{r} 1 \\ 56 \\ +27 \\ \hline 83 \end{array}$$

Now we can add the tens remembering to count the 1 ten that we regrouped from the ones.

1 + 5 + 2 = 8   and   56 + 27 = 83

Exercise

Add. Regroup as necessary.

1.	2.	3.	4.	5.
$\begin{array}{r} 37 \\ +25 \\ \hline \end{array}$	$\begin{array}{r} 48 \\ +37 \\ \hline \end{array}$	$\begin{array}{r} 26 \\ +54 \\ \hline \end{array}$	$\begin{array}{r} 35 \\ +29 \\ \hline \end{array}$	$\begin{array}{r} 54 \\ +18 \\ \hline \end{array}$

Problem Solving

Read the word problem.
Then write the addition problem and find the answer.

6. Mr. McMahon sold 39 hot dogs during the
    first game and 46 during the second.
    How many hot dogs did he sell?   _____

Exercise

Add.

1. 62
    +29

2. 29
    +28

3. 38
    +37

4. 47
    +25

5. 63
    +27

6. 79
    +19

7. 64
    +17

8. 58
    +26

9. 45
    +18

10. 27
    +57

11. 44
    +29

12. 36
    +36

13. 77
    +17

14. 49
    +48

15. 26
    +37

16. 73
    +19

17. 18
    +28

18. 15
    +47

19. 29
    +27

Problem Solving

Read each word problem.
Then write the addition problem and find the answer.

20. Mr. Jones sowed 82 acres of wheat
    and 59 acres of barley. How many
    acres of grain did he sow altogether?   _____

21. The St. John's basketball team scored
    35 points in the first half and 27 points
    in the second half. How many points
    did they score for the whole game?   _____

Adding 3-Digit Numbers With Regrouping

When adding whole numbers we always start with the ones place.

Add: 563 + 362

First we rewrite vertically:
```
 563
+362
```
Make sure all the places are lined up with one another.

As always, we start by adding the ones:

```
 563
+ 362
    5
```

3 + 2 is 5 and we put the 5 in the ones place.

Then we add the tens:

6 tens + 6 tens is 12 tens.

How do we write 12 in the tens place?

We can't so we **regroup**.

```
  1
 563
+362
  25
```

12 tens is the same as 1 hundred and 2 tens.

We put the 1 hundred at the top of the hundreds place and we put the 2 tens in the tens place.

```
  1
 563
+362
 925
```

Now we can add the hundreds remembering to count the 1 hundred that we regrouped from the tens.

1 + 5 + 3 = 9   and   563 + 362 = 925

Exercise

Add. Regroup as necessary.

1. 374
   +253

2. 482
   +375

3. 263
   +542

4. 355
   +291

5. 546
   +152

6. 622
   +292

Adding 4-Digit Numbers With Regrouping

No matter how large the numbers are, we always start with the ones place.

Add: **3446 + 5612**

First we rewrite vertically:
$$\begin{array}{r} 3446 \\ +5612 \\ \hline \end{array}$$

Make sure all the places are lined up with one another.

Then we start with the ones and move left.

Add the ones.	Add the tens	Add the hundreds	Add the thousands
$$\begin{array}{r} 344\textbf{6} \\ +561\textbf{2} \\ \hline 8 \end{array}$$	$$\begin{array}{r} 34\textbf{4}6 \\ +56\textbf{1}2 \\ \hline 58 \end{array}$$	$$\begin{array}{r} {}^{1} \\ 3\textbf{4}46 \\ +5\textbf{6}12 \\ \hline 058 \end{array}$$	$$\begin{array}{r} {}^{1} \\ \textbf{3}446 \\ +\textbf{5}612 \\ \hline 9058 \end{array}$$
6 + 2 = 8 no regrouping necessary	4 + 1 = 5 no regrouping necessary	6 + 4 = 10 must regroup 10 hundreds is 1 thousand and 0 hundreds	1+ 3 + 5 = 9 include regrouping from the hundreds

Exercise

Add. Regroup as necessary.

1. $$\begin{array}{r} 1860 \\ +5525 \\ \hline \end{array}$$
2. $$\begin{array}{r} 2835 \\ +2453 \\ \hline \end{array}$$
3. $$\begin{array}{r} 3844 \\ +3723 \\ \hline \end{array}$$
4. $$\begin{array}{r} 4862 \\ +4314 \\ \hline \end{array}$$

5. $$\begin{array}{r} 2645 \\ +6652 \\ \hline \end{array}$$
6. $$\begin{array}{r} 1943 \\ +5423 \\ \hline \end{array}$$
7. $$\begin{array}{r} 5751 \\ +2933 \\ \hline \end{array}$$
8. $$\begin{array}{r} 4516 \\ +3620 \\ \hline \end{array}$$

9. $$\begin{array}{r} 3542 \\ +5630 \\ \hline \end{array}$$
10. $$\begin{array}{r} 4714 \\ +2832 \\ \hline \end{array}$$
11. $$\begin{array}{r} 3141 \\ +3927 \\ \hline \end{array}$$
12. $$\begin{array}{r} 2954 \\ +5924 \\ \hline \end{array}$$

Addition With More Regroupings

Sometimes we will need to regroup more than once.

Add: 467 + 395

First we rewrite vertically:
$$
\begin{array}{r}
467 \\
+\ 395 \\
\hline
\end{array}
$$
Make sure all the places are lined up with one another.

Then we start with the ones and move left.

Add the ones.	Add the tens.	Add the hundreds.
$\begin{array}{r} 1 \\ 467 \\ +\ 395 \\ \hline 2 \end{array}$	$\begin{array}{r} 1\,1 \\ 467 \\ +\ 395 \\ \hline 62 \end{array}$	$\begin{array}{r} 11 \\ 467 \\ +\ 395 \\ \hline 862 \end{array}$
7 + 5 = 12 must regroup 12 ones is 1 ten and 2 ones	1+ 6 + 9 = 16 include regrouping from the ones must regroup 16 tens is 1 hundred and 6 tens	1+ 4 + 3 = 8 include regrouping from the tens

Add: 3786 + 4645

Add the ones.	Add the tens.	Add the hundreds.	Add the thousands.
$\begin{array}{r} 1 \\ 3786 \\ +4645 \\ \hline 1 \end{array}$	$\begin{array}{r} 1\,1 \\ 3786 \\ +4645 \\ \hline 31 \end{array}$	$\begin{array}{r} 1\,11 \\ 3786 \\ +4645 \\ \hline 431 \end{array}$	$\begin{array}{r} 111 \\ 3786 \\ +4645 \\ \hline 8431 \end{array}$
6 + 5 = 11 must regroup 11 ones is 1 ten and 1 one	1+ 8 + 4 = 13 include regrouping from the ones must regroup 13 tens is 1 hundred and 3 tens	1+ 7 + 6 = 14 include regrouping from the tens must regroup 14 hundreds is 1 thousand and 4 hundreds	1+ 3 + 4 = 8 include regrouping from the hundreds

Exercise

Add. Regroup as necessary.

1. 74
    +62

2. 56
    +93

3. 49
    +60

4. 94
    +68

5. 77
    +46

6. 694
    + 268

7. 477
    + 346

8. 259
    + 375

9. 572
    + 238

10. 343
     + 599

11. 466
     + 285

12. 1787
     +2585

13. 2639
     +4892

14. 4366
     +3846

15. 7447
     +1978

16. 7875
     +1855

17. 6589
     +1696

Problem Solving

Read each word problem.
Then write the addition problem and find the answer.

18. John took the first part of the test in 56 minutes.
     He took the second part in 58 minutes.
     How many minutes did he spend on the two tests? _____

19. It is 3,768 paces from the back porch to the
     black rock and 2,986 paces from there to the
     secret fort. How many paces is it from the back
     porch to the black rock to the secret fort? _____

Problem Solving

Read each word problem.
Then write the addition problem and find the answer.

1. There were 627 potatoes in the large
   bin and 297 potatoes in the smaller bin.
   How many potatoes were in both bins? _____

2. Mr. Forrest drove 366 miles on the first day
   and 259 miles on the second day. How many
   miles did he drive both days? _____

3. Martha collected 731 points for the computer
   project. Her brother James was only able to
   collect 169 points. How many points did they
   collect together? _____

4. There were 446 jelly beans in one container
   and 473 jelly beans in another. How many
   jelly beans were there in the 2 containers? _____

5. A small pickup could carry 1,986 pounds of
   cargo. A larger truck could carry 7,123 pounds
   of cargo. How much cargo could the two trucks
   carry altogether? _____

6. The River Blue is 3,850 kilometers long. It's
   main tributary is 2,465 kilometers long. How
   many kilometers long are the two rivers together? _____

7. The St. Ambrose third graders collected 2794 labels
   in March and then collected 5739 labels in April.
   How many labels did they collect in March and April? _____

8. The apple pickers divided into two groups. The first
   group picked 2357 apples and the second group picked
   3456 apples. How many apples did the two groups pick? _____

Column Addition – Three or More Addends

Sometimes we need to find the sum of more than two addends.

Mr. Hawbaker was visiting churches in Montana. He drove 223 miles from Billings to Butte, to see the giant statue of Our Lady of the Rockies and then he drove another 71 miles to the St. Helena Cathedral. The next day he drove 114 miles to Missoula. The following day he returned 340 miles to Billings. How many miles did he travel in the three days?

From Billings to Butte is _____ miles.

From Butte to Helena is _____ miles.

From Helena to Missoula is _____ miles.

From Missoula to Billings is _____ miles.

Add: 223 + 71 + 114 + 340

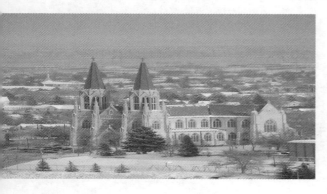

First we rewrite vertically:

Make sure all the places are lined up with one another.

$$\begin{array}{r} 223 \\ 71 \\ 114 \\ +340 \\ \hline \end{array}$$

Then we start with the ones and move left.

Add the ones. Regroup if needed.	Add the tens. Regroup if needed.	Add the hundreds. Regroup if needed.
$\begin{array}{r} 223 \\ 71 \\ 114 \\ +340 \\ \hline 8 \end{array}$	$\begin{array}{r} {}^{1} \\ 223 \\ 71 \\ 114 \\ +340 \\ \hline 48 \end{array}$	$\begin{array}{r} {}^{1} \\ 223 \\ 71 \\ 114 \\ +340 \\ \hline 748 \end{array}$
3 + 1 + 4 + 0 = 8 no regroup necessary	2 + 7 + 1 + 4 = 14 regroup 14 tens to 1 hundred and 4 tens	1 + 2 + 1 + 3 = 7 no regroup necessary

Exercise

Column Addition

Add. Regroup as necessary.

1.
```
  421
  145
  162
+ 231
```

2.
```
  178
  214
  103
+ 407
```

3.
```
  513
  223
  641
+ 412
```

4.
```
  421
  372
  635
+ 444
```

5.
```
 3723
 4564
 1748
+4257
```

6.
```
 7289
 3652
 4287
+4218
```

7.
```
 1454
 1323
 2317
+6035
```

8.
```
  223
 2545
  199
+3162
```

9.
```
 2225
   85
  425
+5424
```

10.
```
  631
 4316
  211
+7312
```

11.
```
 6135
 5743
 1424
+2816
```

12.
```
   56
  240
 6355
+2143
```

13.
```
 2923
 4254
 6787
+3926
```

14.
```
 2245
   45
 3056
+ 524
```

15. Billings has a population of 89,847. Missoula has a population of 57,053. Great Falls has 56,690 people. Helena has a population of 25,780 and Butte has 33,892 people. What is the population of all five cities? _____

Adding Money

The first thing to do when adding money is to line up the dollars $ and cents ¢.

Add: $6.49 + $8.98

First we rewrite vertically:

$$\begin{array}{r} \$6.49 \\ +\ 8.98 \\ \hline \end{array}$$

Make sure to line up the dollars and cents.

Then we add as usual.

$$\begin{array}{r} {\scriptstyle 1\ 1} \\ \$6.49 \\ +\ 8.98 \\ \hline 15\ 47 \end{array}$$

Then write the $ and . in the sum.

$$\begin{array}{r} \$6.49 \\ +\ 8.98 \\ \hline \$15.47 \end{array}$$

Exercise

Add. Regroup as necessary.

1.
$$\begin{array}{r} \$8.75 \\ +\ 1.46 \\ \hline \end{array}$$

2.
$$\begin{array}{r} \$3.27 \\ +\ 1.35 \\ \hline \end{array}$$

3.
$$\begin{array}{r} \$4.91 \\ +\ 4.75 \\ \hline \end{array}$$

4.
$$\begin{array}{r} \$3.00 \\ +\ 5.00 \\ \hline \end{array}$$

5.
$$\begin{array}{r} \$3.36 \\ +\ 4.58 \\ \hline \end{array}$$

6.
$$\begin{array}{r} \$6.37 \\ +\ 1.67 \\ \hline \end{array}$$

7.
$$\begin{array}{r} \$5.78 \\ +\ 2.64 \\ \hline \end{array}$$

8.
$$\begin{array}{r} \$2.49 \\ +\ 4.98 \\ \hline \end{array}$$

9. Stephen spent $5.79 on a prayer book and $3.99 on a rosary. How much did he spend? _____

10. Kevin bought a toolbox for $12.49 and Laura bought a paint set for $14.59. How much did they spend altogether? _____

Add. Regroup as necessary.

1. $9.15
    + 7.36

2. $5.88
    + 3.99

3. $4.23
    + 9.84

4. $7.95
    + 5.39

5. $7.25
    + 2.36

6. $2.79
    + 2.62

7. $1.65
    + 8.36

8. $3.50
    + 6.45

9. $3.75
    + 4.55

10. $8.53
    + 1.65

11. $6.37
    + 4.96

12. $2.48
    + 3.85

13. $7.56
    + 6.48

14. $2.46
    + 5.59

15. $5.51
    + 4.66

16. $2.85
    + 6.35

17. David paid $8.43 for a hammer and
    $5.77 for a saw. How much did he pay
    for them altogether? _____

18. Helen spent $5.88 at the carnival and then spent
    $2.66 for food. How much did she spend altogether? _____

19. Maria received $7.22 from one customer
    and $9.67 from another. How much did
    she receive altogether? _____

20. Jacob made a profit of $7.89 on a sale and
    a profit of $9.59 on another sale. How much
    did he profit altogether? _____

Add. Regroup as necessary.

1. $\begin{array}{r} 45 \\ +19 \\ \hline \end{array}$

2. $\begin{array}{r} 28 \\ +63 \\ \hline \end{array}$

3. $\begin{array}{r} 57 \\ +23 \\ \hline \end{array}$

4. $\begin{array}{r} 67 \\ +28 \\ \hline \end{array}$

5. $\begin{array}{r} 39 \\ +46 \\ \hline \end{array}$

6. $\begin{array}{r} 628 \\ +\ 196 \\ \hline \end{array}$

7. $\begin{array}{r} 427 \\ +\ 277 \\ \hline \end{array}$

8. $\begin{array}{r} 259 \\ +\ 442 \\ \hline \end{array}$

9. $\begin{array}{r} 155 \\ +\ 156 \\ \hline \end{array}$

10. $\begin{array}{r} 285 \\ +\ 476 \\ \hline \end{array}$

11. $\begin{array}{r} 7621 \\ +1596 \\ \hline \end{array}$

12. $\begin{array}{r} 3428 \\ +2596 \\ \hline \end{array}$

13. $\begin{array}{r} 485 \\ +\ 346 \\ \hline \end{array}$

14. $\begin{array}{r} 754 \\ +\ 196 \\ \hline \end{array}$

15. $\begin{array}{r} 1847 \\ +7697 \\ \hline \end{array}$

16. $\begin{array}{r} 1996 \\ +4283 \\ \hline \end{array}$

17. $\begin{array}{r} 128 \\ 376 \\ 532 \\ +\ 111 \\ \hline \end{array}$

18. $\begin{array}{r} 586 \\ 428 \\ 821 \\ +\ 764 \\ \hline \end{array}$

19. $\begin{array}{r} 2295 \\ 1876 \\ 1381 \\ +1003 \\ \hline \end{array}$

20. $\begin{array}{r} 8654 \\ 1298 \\ 1385 \\ +1830 \\ \hline \end{array}$

21. $\begin{array}{r} \$9.83 \\ +\ 1.79 \\ \hline \end{array}$

22. $\begin{array}{r} \$8.85 \\ +\ 5.91 \\ \hline \end{array}$

23. $\begin{array}{r} \$6.73 \\ +\ 3.82 \\ \hline \end{array}$

24. $\begin{array}{r} \$3.96 \\ +\ 5.48 \\ \hline \end{array}$

25. $\begin{array}{r} \$7.16 \\ +\ 1.93 \\ \hline \end{array}$

26. $\begin{array}{r} \$1.83 \\ +\ 7.39 \\ \hline \end{array}$

27. $\begin{array}{r} \$2.95 \\ +\ 5.76 \\ \hline \end{array}$

28. $\begin{array}{r} \$4.09 \\ +\ 4.91 \\ \hline \end{array}$

Read each word problem.
Then write the addition problem and find the answer.

1. There were 627 peanuts in the larger bag
    and 297 peanuts in the smaller bag.
    How many peanuts were in both bags?   _____

2. Jane picked 366 apples in the morning and
    259 apples in the afternoon. How many apples
    did she pick in the day?   _____

3. There were 731 coconuts strewn about
    the beach after the storm. There were
    also 169 fallen mangoes. How many
    coconuts and mangoes were there altogether?   _____

4. It is 446 miles from here to Cedarville and
    473 miles from Cedarville to Oakwood. How
    many miles is it from here to Oakwood?   _____

5. Farmer Jones had 4 vegetable fields. There
    were 1986 rutabagas growing in one field.
    There were 7123 turnips in another field.
    Another field had 1986 parsnips in it and
    the last field had 7123 sugar beets. How many
    vegetables were there growing in all 4 fields?   _____

6. There were 3850 thingamajigs and 1986 gizmos
    along with 7123 widgets and 2465 thingamabobs.
    How many thingamajigs, gizmos, widgets,
    and thingamabobs were there altogether?   _____

7. Mom and Aunt Martha went out to lunch.
    Mom's meal cost $6.32 and Aunt Martha's
    cost $7.79. How much did they cost together?   _____

If you have not already done so, complete the Skills Test for Objective #4 on pp. 194-195. When you have successfully completed the test, you may check it off on your objectives list on page 185.

Subtracting Whole Numbers With More Than One Digit

When subtracting whole numbers we always start with the ones place.

Subtract: 879 − 352

First we rewrite vertically:

$$\begin{array}{r} 879 \\ -\,352 \\ \hline \end{array}$$

Make sure the ones, tens and hundreds are lined up with one another.

Subtract the ones.	Subtract the tens.	Subtract the hundreds.
$$\begin{array}{r} 879 \\ -\,352 \\ \hline 7 \end{array}$$	$$\begin{array}{r} 879 \\ -\,352 \\ \hline 27 \end{array}$$	$$\begin{array}{r} 879 \\ -\,352 \\ \hline 527 \end{array}$$
$9 - 2 = 7$ no regroup necessary	$7 - 5 = 2$ no regroup necessary	$8 - 3 = 5$ no regroup necessary

Subtraction

Exercise

Subtract.

1. $$\begin{array}{r} 546 \\ -\,232 \\ \hline \end{array}$$
2. $$\begin{array}{r} 693 \\ -\,242 \\ \hline \end{array}$$
3. $$\begin{array}{r} 378 \\ -\,212 \\ \hline \end{array}$$
4. $$\begin{array}{r} 889 \\ -\,242 \\ \hline \end{array}$$

5. $$\begin{array}{r} 938 \\ -\,213 \\ \hline \end{array}$$
6. $$\begin{array}{r} 872 \\ -\,371 \\ \hline \end{array}$$
7. $$\begin{array}{r} 285 \\ -\,133 \\ \hline \end{array}$$
8. $$\begin{array}{r} 548 \\ -\,342 \\ \hline \end{array}$$

9. $$\begin{array}{r} 875 \\ -\,262 \\ \hline \end{array}$$
10. $$\begin{array}{r} 545 \\ -\,214 \\ \hline \end{array}$$
11. $$\begin{array}{r} 503 \\ -\,401 \\ \hline \end{array}$$
12. $$\begin{array}{r} 377 \\ -\,107 \\ \hline \end{array}$$

13. I am reading a 364-page book.
    I have finished 123 pages.
    How many pages are left?   _____

Regroup 1 ten for 10 ones

32 = _____ tens _____ ones

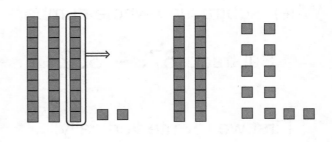

We want to take one of the tens
and move it to the ones column.

Now instead of 3 tens and 2 ones,
we have 2 tens and 12 ones

32 = ___2___ tens ___12___ ones

Now try regrouping 1 ten for 10 ones **and** 1 hundred for 10 tens.

First, the tens for the ones.

463 = ___4___ hundreds ___5___ tens ___13___ ones

Then, the hundreds for the tens.

= ___3___ hundreds ___15___ tens ___13___ ones

Exercise

Regroup 1 ten for 10 ones

43 = _____ tens _____ ones

75 = _____ tens _____ ones

94 = _____ tens _____ ones

Regroup 1 ten for 10 ones **and** 1 hundred for 10 tens.

634 = _____ hundreds _____ tens _____ ones

= _____ hundreds _____ tens _____ ones

Subtracting With Regrouping

Subtract: 582 − 359

First we rewrite vertically:

$$\begin{array}{r} 582 \\ -359 \\ \hline \end{array}$$

Make sure the ones, tens and hundreds are lined up with one another.

We will be checking at each step to see if we need to regroup.

Subtract the ones.

2 − 9   ?

Do we need to regroup? Yes, so regroup 1 ten as 10 ones and add them to the ones place and change the digit in the tens place to 1 less.

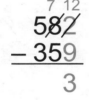

$$\begin{array}{r} {}^{7}\,{}^{12} \\ 58\!\!\!/2\!\!\!/ \\ -359 \\ \hline 3 \end{array}$$

12 − 9 = 3
move to the tens ↗

Subtract the tens.

7 − 5   ?

Do we need to regroup? No. Subtract.

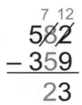

$$\begin{array}{r} {}^{7}\,{}^{12} \\ 58\!\!\!/2\!\!\!/ \\ -359 \\ \hline 23 \end{array}$$

7 − 5 = 2
move to the hundreds ↗

Subtract the hundreds.

$$\begin{array}{r} {}^{7}\,{}^{12} \\ 58\!\!\!/2\!\!\!/ \\ -359 \\ \hline 223 \end{array}$$

5 − 3 = 2

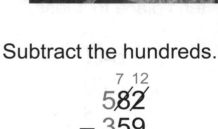

Exercise

Subtract. Regroup as necessary.

1. $\begin{array}{r} 738 \\ -254 \\ \hline \end{array}$
2. $\begin{array}{r} 859 \\ -492 \\ \hline \end{array}$
3. $\begin{array}{r} 926 \\ -245 \\ \hline \end{array}$
4. $\begin{array}{r} 647 \\ -564 \\ \hline \end{array}$

5. $\begin{array}{r} 787 \\ -438 \\ \hline \end{array}$
6. $\begin{array}{r} 354 \\ -261 \\ \hline \end{array}$
7. $\begin{array}{r} 783 \\ -249 \\ \hline \end{array}$
8. $\begin{array}{r} 895 \\ -429 \\ \hline \end{array}$

Subtracting With More Regroupings

Subtract: 641 − 278

First we rewrite vertically:

Make sure the ones, tens, and
hundreds are lined up with one another.

We will be checking at each step
to see if we need to regroup

$$\begin{array}{r} 641 \\ -278 \\ \hline \end{array}$$

Subtract the ones.

1 − 8   ?

Do we need to regroup?
Yes, so regroup 1 ten
as 10 ones, add them
to the ones place, and
change the digit in the
tens place to 1 less.

$$\begin{array}{r} {\scriptstyle 3\;11} \\ 6\cancel{4}\cancel{1} \\ -278 \\ \hline 3 \end{array}$$

11 − 8 = 3
move to the tens ↗

Subtract the tens.

3 − 7   ?

Do we need to regroup?
Yes, so regroup 1 hundred as
10 tens, add them to the tens
place, and change the digit in
the hundreds place to 1 less.

$$\begin{array}{r} {\scriptstyle 5\;\cancel{3}\;11} \\ 6\cancel{4}\cancel{1} \\ -278 \\ \hline 63 \end{array}$$

13 − 7 = 6
move to the hundreds ↗

Subtract the
hundreds.

$$\begin{array}{r} {\scriptstyle 5\;\cancel{3}\;11} \\ \cancel{6}\cancel{4}\cancel{1} \\ -278 \\ \hline 363 \end{array}$$

5 − 2 = 3

Exercise

Subtract. Regroup as necessary.

1.
$$\begin{array}{r} 735 \\ -259 \\ \hline \end{array}$$

2.
$$\begin{array}{r} 852 \\ -494 \\ \hline \end{array}$$

3.
$$\begin{array}{r} 924 \\ -246 \\ \hline \end{array}$$

4.
$$\begin{array}{r} 647 \\ -568 \\ \hline \end{array}$$

5.
$$\begin{array}{r} 778 \\ -488 \\ \hline \end{array}$$

6.
$$\begin{array}{r} 886 \\ -388 \\ \hline \end{array}$$

7.
$$\begin{array}{r} 525 \\ -188 \\ \hline \end{array}$$

8.
$$\begin{array}{r} 757 \\ -389 \\ \hline \end{array}$$

Exercise

Subtract. Regroup as necessary.

1. 470
    − 391

2. 606
    − 119

3. 864
    − 598

4. 942
    − 488

5. 350
    − 265

6. 906
    − 557

7. 561
    − 276

8. 410
    − 168

9. 501
    − 385

10. 615
    − 156

11. 834
    − 256

12. 945
    − 169

13. 653
    − 397

14. 730
    − 178

15. 802
    − 285

16. 923
    − 355

17. James picked 545 strawberries and his
    little brother Michael picked 268 strawberries.
    How many more strawberries did James pick?   _____

18. The trip was 352 miles long.
    185 miles were on the interstate.
    How many miles were not on the interstate?   _____

19. There were 226 contestants in the
    Spelling Bee. After the first 5 rounds
    152 contestants had been eliminated.
    How many contestants were left after 5 rounds?   _____

Subtract: **8462 − 4784**

First we rewrite vertically:

$$\begin{array}{r} 8462 \\ -\,4784 \\ \hline \end{array}$$

Make sure all the places are lined up with one another.

We will be checking at each step to see if we need to regroup.

Subtract the ones.

2 − 4   ?

Do we need to regroup?
Yes, so regroup 1 ten as 10 ones,
add them to the ones place and
change the digit in the tens place to
1 less.

$$\begin{array}{r} {\scriptstyle 5\ \ 12} \\ 846\cancel{2} \\ -\,4784 \\ \hline 8 \end{array}$$

12 − 4 = 8
move to the tens ↗

Subtract the tens.

5 − 8   ?

Do we need to regroup?
Yes, so regroup 1 hundred as
10 tens, add them to the tens
place and change the digit in the
hundreds place to 1 less.

$$\begin{array}{r} {\scriptstyle \ \ 15} \\ {\scriptstyle 3\ \cancel{5}\ 12} \\ 84\cancel{6}\cancel{2} \\ -\,4784 \\ \hline 78 \end{array}$$

15 − 8 = 7
↙ move to the hundreds

Subtract the hundreds.

3 − 7   ?

Do we need to regroup?
Yes, so regroup 1 thousand as
10 hundreds, add them to the
hundreds place and change the
digit in the thousands place to 1 less.

$$\begin{array}{r} {\scriptstyle 13\ 15} \\ {\scriptstyle 7\ \cancel{8}\ \cancel{5}\ 12} \\ 8\cancel{4}\cancel{6}\cancel{2} \\ -\,4784 \\ \hline 678 \end{array}$$

13 − 7 = 6
move to the thousands ↗

Subtract the thousands.

$$\begin{array}{r} {\scriptstyle 13\ 15} \\ {\scriptstyle 7\ \cancel{8}\ \cancel{5}\ 12} \\ \cancel{8}462 \\ -\,4784 \\ \hline 3678 \end{array}$$

7 − 4 = 3

Exercise

Subtract. Regroup as necessary.

1.
```
  52
- 18
```

2.
```
  47
- 39
```

3.
```
  568
- 299
```

4.
```
  381
- 198
```

5.
```
  5681
- 2998
```

6.
```
  3814
- 1986
```

7.
```
  3152
- 1885
```

8.
```
  4345
- 1568
```

9.
```
  3752
- 2985
```

10.
```
  2626
- 1959
```

11.
```
  5568
- 3699
```

12.
```
  4381
- 2798
```

13.
```
  2813
- 1985
```

14.
```
  4237
- 2459
```

15.
```
  5676
- 3699
```

16.
```
  4165
- 2796
```

17. Mr. Houlihan had 536 head of cattle.
He sold 158 head at market.
How many head of cattle did he have left? _____

18. There were 5434 things that could have gone
wrong but only 3769 things did actually go
wrong. How many things did not go wrong? _____

19. Robert saw 862 birds and Carl saw
786 birds. How many more birds
did Robert see than Carl? _____

Exercise

Subtract. Regroup as necessary.

1.
$$\begin{array}{r} 54 \\ - \ 37 \\ \hline \end{array}$$

2.
$$\begin{array}{r} 63 \\ - \ 26 \\ \hline \end{array}$$

3.
$$\begin{array}{r} 8354 \\ - \ 2586 \\ \hline \end{array}$$

4.
$$\begin{array}{r} 9425 \\ - \ 1659 \\ \hline \end{array}$$

5.
$$\begin{array}{r} 848 \\ - \ 599 \\ \hline \end{array}$$

6.
$$\begin{array}{r} 285 \\ - \ 197 \\ \hline \end{array}$$

7.
$$\begin{array}{r} 7584 \\ - \ 1675 \\ \hline \end{array}$$

8.
$$\begin{array}{r} 6563 \\ - \ 3997 \\ \hline \end{array}$$

9.
$$\begin{array}{r} 7380 \\ - \ 1798 \\ \hline \end{array}$$

10.
$$\begin{array}{r} 8012 \\ - \ 2885 \\ \hline \end{array}$$

11.
$$\begin{array}{r} 9234 \\ - \ 3556 \\ \hline \end{array}$$

12.
$$\begin{array}{r} 3540 \\ - \ 2665 \\ \hline \end{array}$$

13. Of the 357 apples, 179 were rotten. How many were not rotten? _____

14. The company had an order for 5475 widgets. They had 2698 widgets in stock. How many more widgets did they need to make? _____

15. During the blood drive 274 people donated blood. Of those, 197 people had O+ blood type. How many people were not O+ blood type? _____

16. George had 543 marbles and he gave 376 to his brother, Richard. How many marbles does George have now? _____

17. There were 2256 available tickets. Then 1569 of the tickets were sold. How many tickets were left to sell? _____

Objective #5 – Subtraction of Whole Numbers

The student will be able to subtract up to 4-digit whole numbers and will demonstrate his mastery by completing the Skill Test for Objective #5 on pp. 196-197 quickly and accurately.

Subtracting Problem Solving

Subtracting Money

The first thing to do when subtracting money is to line up the dollars and cents.

Subtract: **$85.98 – $59.79**

First we rewrite vertically:

$$\begin{array}{r} \$\ 85.98 \\ -\ 59.79 \\ \hline \end{array}$$

Make sure to line up the dollars and cents.

Then we subtract as usual regrouping if necessary.

$$\begin{array}{r} {\scriptstyle 7\ 15\ 8\ 18} \\ \$\ \cancel{85.98} \\ -\ 59.79 \\ \hline 26\ 19 \end{array}$$

Then write the $ and . in the difference.

$$\begin{array}{r} \$\ 85.98 \\ -\ 59.79 \\ \hline \$\ 26.19 \end{array}$$

Exercise

Subtract. Regroup as necessary.

1. $$\begin{array}{r} \$\ 3.67 \\ -\ 1.88 \\ \hline \end{array}$$

2. $$\begin{array}{r} \$\ 6.78 \\ -\ 1.98 \\ \hline \end{array}$$

3. $$\begin{array}{r} \$\ 5.21 \\ -\ 1.73 \\ \hline \end{array}$$

4. $$\begin{array}{r} \$\ 5.10 \\ -\ 2.36 \\ \hline \end{array}$$

5. $$\begin{array}{r} \$\ 38.43 \\ -\ 19.69 \\ \hline \end{array}$$

6. $$\begin{array}{r} \$\ 74.32 \\ -\ 26.97 \\ \hline \end{array}$$

7. $$\begin{array}{r} \$\ 93.46 \\ -\ 89.69 \\ \hline \end{array}$$

8. $$\begin{array}{r} \$\ 82.17 \\ -\ 57.39 \\ \hline \end{array}$$

9. Jim bought a golf club for $72.84. His brother found the same club on sale for $44.96. How much more did Jim pay than his brother?

   _____

Exercise

Subtract. Regroup as necessary.

1. $ 75.23
    − 34.14

2. $ 67.33
    − 42.43

3. $ 58.35
    − 19.39

4. $ 76.50
    − 48.92

5. $ 60.56
    − 32.98

6. $ 47.23
    − 22.21

7. $ 58.06
    − 24.47

8. $ 39.24
    − 11.63

9. $ 78.11
    − 29.12

10. $ 64.25
    − 35.87

11. $ 53.46
    − 27.35

12. $ 26.38
    − 15.49

13. $ 75.85
    − 43.96

14. $ 45.06
    − 26.17

15. $ 53.64
    − 34.74

16. $ 27.40
    − 15.41

17. The whole meal cost $3.62. The drink
    and the fries cost $1.74. How much
    was the rest of the meal?

18. The full price of the ticket was $9.00 but
    Grace got a discount and only had to pay
    $7.50. How much did she save?

19. The price of the doohickey was $9.45.
    The doodad only cost $4.63. How much
    more did the doohickey cost than the doodad?

20. The price of the basketball goal was $94.48.
    Timothy and George have saved $25.67.
    How much more do they need for the goal?

Subtracting Money

Review

Subtract. Regroup as necessary.

1. 84
    − 59

2. 28
    − 19

3. 9056
    − 5597

4. 5631
    − 2776

5. $ 41.00
    − 16.88

6. $ 50.21
    − 38.55

7. $ 61.50
    − 15.65

8. $ 52.05
    − 19.76

9. 7567
    − 3879

10. $ 54.34
    − 37.69

11. 4710
    − 3961

12. $ 27.43
    − 19.99

13. 6006
    − 1189

14. 8614
    − 5958

15. 9425
    − 4888

16. 3574
    − 1797

17. The stamp album can hold 504 stamps.
    Thomas has placed 235 stamps.
    How many more stamps does he have room for?   _____

18. The two brothers bought lunch for themselves
    for a total of $6.72. One of the boy's meal cost
    $2.85. How much did the other one cost?   _____

19. A long journey is 8922 miles. After you
    have traveled 2847 miles, how many more
    miles do you have to go to journey's end?

20. Jane wants a book for $5.62. She has
    $3.57. How much more does she need?

If you have not already done so, complete the Skills Test for Objective #5 on pp. 196-197. When you have successfully completed the test you may check it off on your objectives list on page 185.

Facts Check

Add.

1. $\begin{array}{r} 3 \\ +2 \\ \hline \end{array}$
2. $\begin{array}{r} 5 \\ +7 \\ \hline \end{array}$
3. $\begin{array}{r} 6 \\ +9 \\ \hline \end{array}$
4. $\begin{array}{r} 9 \\ +9 \\ \hline \end{array}$
5. $\begin{array}{r} 4 \\ +5 \\ \hline \end{array}$
6. $\begin{array}{r} 8 \\ +5 \\ \hline \end{array}$

Subtract.

7. $\begin{array}{r} 13 \\ -9 \\ \hline \end{array}$
8. $\begin{array}{r} 9 \\ -3 \\ \hline \end{array}$
9. $\begin{array}{r} 11 \\ -8 \\ \hline \end{array}$
10. $\begin{array}{r} 14 \\ -6 \\ \hline \end{array}$
11. $\begin{array}{r} 9 \\ -4 \\ \hline \end{array}$
12. $\begin{array}{r} 10 \\ -7 \\ \hline \end{array}$

Multiply.

13. $\begin{array}{r} 6 \\ \times 9 \\ \hline \end{array}$
14. $\begin{array}{r} 0 \\ \times 5 \\ \hline \end{array}$
15. $\begin{array}{r} 7 \\ \times 4 \\ \hline \end{array}$
16. $\begin{array}{r} 5 \\ \times 5 \\ \hline \end{array}$
17. $\begin{array}{r} 3 \\ \times 6 \\ \hline \end{array}$
18. $\begin{array}{r} 6 \\ \times 6 \\ \hline \end{array}$

19. $\begin{array}{r} 9 \\ \times 7 \\ \hline \end{array}$
20. $\begin{array}{r} 3 \\ \times 2 \\ \hline \end{array}$
21. $\begin{array}{r} 5 \\ \times 4 \\ \hline \end{array}$
22. $\begin{array}{r} 7 \\ \times 9 \\ \hline \end{array}$
23. $\begin{array}{r} 4 \\ \times 8 \\ \hline \end{array}$
24. $\begin{array}{r} 8 \\ \times 7 \\ \hline \end{array}$

25. $\begin{array}{r} 2 \\ \times 6 \\ \hline \end{array}$
26. $\begin{array}{r} 4 \\ \times 4 \\ \hline \end{array}$
27. $\begin{array}{r} 5 \\ \times 9 \\ \hline \end{array}$
28. $\begin{array}{r} 6 \\ \times 7 \\ \hline \end{array}$
29. $\begin{array}{r} 7 \\ \times 2 \\ \hline \end{array}$
30. $\begin{array}{r} 9 \\ \times 6 \\ \hline \end{array}$

Divide.

31. $24 \div 4 = $ _____
32. $4\overline{)32}$
33. $10 \div 2 = $ _____
34. $3\overline{)6}$

35. $12 \div 4 = $ _____
36. $8\overline{)16}$
37. $36 \div 9 = $ _____
38. $9\overline{)27}$

39. $21 \div 7 = $ _____
40. $7\overline{)14}$
41. $72 \div 9 = $ _____
42. $9\overline{)81}$

Multiplication

In multiplication, we need to pay very close attention to place value.

Let's look at what happens when we multiply by 1, 10, 100, and 1,000.

We will use the number 5 for an example. We know from the Identity Property that when we multiply by 1 the product is the other factor.

$$5 \times 1 = 5$$

When we multiply by a multiple of 10, 100, or 1,000 we simply add zeros for the correct place value.
Look at the patterns:

$5 \times 1 = 5$ $5 \times 5 = 25$
$5 \times 10 = 50$ $5 \times 50 = 250$
$5 \times 100 = 500$ $5 \times 500 = 2,500$
$5 \times 1000 = 5,000$ $5 \times 5000 = 25,000$

$3 \times 1 = 3$ $3 \times 3 = 9$
$3 \times 10 = 30$ $3 \times 30 = 90$
$3 \times 100 = 300$ $3 \times 300 = 900$
$3 \times 1000 = 3,000$ $3 \times 3000 = 9,000$

Exercise

Complete the pattern.

1. $7 \times 1 =$ _____

     $7 \times 10 =$ _____

     $7 \times 100 =$ _____

     $7 \times 1000 =$ _____

2. $7 \times 7 =$ _____

     $7 \times 70 =$ _____

     $7 \times 700 =$ _____

     $7 \times 7000 =$ _____

Complete the pattern.

3. $4 \times 1 =$ _____

 $4 \times 10 =$ _____

 $4 \times 100 =$ _____

 $4 \times 1000 =$ _____

4. $4 \times 4 =$ _____

 $4 \times 40 =$ _____

 $4 \times 400 =$ _____

 $4 \times 4000 =$ _____

5. $8 \times 1 =$ _____

 $8 \times 10 =$ _____

 $8 \times 100 =$ _____

 $8 \times 1000 =$ _____

6. $8 \times 8 =$ _____

 $8 \times 80 =$ _____

 $8 \times 800 =$ _____

 $8 \times 8000 =$ _____

7. $2 \times 1 =$ _____

 $2 \times 10 =$ _____

 $2 \times 100 =$ _____

 $2 \times 1000 =$ _____

8. $2 \times 5 =$ _____

 $2 \times 50 =$ _____

 $2 \times 500 =$ _____

 $2 \times 5000 =$ _____

9. $3 \times 1 =$ _____

 $3 \times 10 =$ _____

 $3 \times 100 =$ _____

 $3 \times 1000 =$ _____

10. $3 \times 6 =$ _____

 $3 \times 60 =$ _____

 $3 \times 600 =$ _____

 $3 \times 6000 =$ _____

Multiplication

Multiplication with Expanded Form

To further explore multiplication and place value, we will begin multiplying numbers in the expanded form. We will use something called the Distributive Property as well, but you need not learn it now.

Look at the following example:

$$32 \times 3 \quad = \quad (30 + 2) \times 3 \quad = \quad 30 \times 3 + 2 \times 3$$
$$= \quad \quad \quad = \quad 90 + 6$$
$$96 \quad = \quad 96 \quad = \quad 96$$

We will multiply some 2 and 3 digit numbers by a 1 digit number. We will write the 2 or 3 digit number in expanded form and then multiply each addend by the one digit number like we did in the last exercise.

Exercise

Rewrite each problem into 2 or 3 problems using the expanded form. Find each product and then find the sum of the products.

Example:
$$\begin{array}{r} 43 \\ \times\ 8 \\ \hline 344 \end{array}$$

$$40 \times 8 = 320$$
$$3 \times 8 = {}^{+}\ 24$$
$$\overline{344}$$

1. $\begin{array}{r} 36 \\ \times\ 7 \end{array}$

_____ × _____ = _____

_____ × _____ = $^{+}$ _____

_____

2. $\begin{array}{r} 243 \\ \times\ 4 \end{array}$

_____ × _____ = _____

_____ × _____ = _____

_____ × _____ = $^{+}$ _____

_____

Multiplication

Rewrite each problem into 2 or 3 problems using the expanded form. Find each product and then find the sum of the products.

3. 27
    × 6   ____ × ____ = ____

             ____ × ____ = **+** ____

                                    ____

4. 189
    × 4   ____ × ____ = ____

             ____ × ____ = ____

             ____ × ____ = **+** ____

                                    ____

5. 14
    × 9   ____ × ____ = ____

             ____ × ____ = **+** ____

                                    ____

6. 42
    × 8   ____ × ____ = ____

             ____ × ____ = **+** ____

                                    ____

7. 146
    × 5   ____ × ____ = ____

             ____ × ____ = ____

             ____ × ____ = **+** ____

                                    ____

Multiplication

3 × 321 =

Multiply ones. 3 × 1 one = 3 ones	Multiply tens. 3 × 2 tens = 6 tens	Multiply hundreds. 3 × 3 hundreds = 9 hundreds

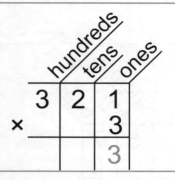

```
  hundreds tens ones          hundreds tens ones          hundreds tens ones
    3    2    1                  3    2    1                  3    2    1
  ×         3                  ×         3                  ×         3
           3                         6    3              9    6    3
```

2 × 234 =

Multiply ones. 2 × 4 ones = 8 ones	Multiply tens. 2 × 3 tens = 6 tens	Multiply hundreds. 2 × 2 hundreds = 4 hundreds

```
   234            234            234
 ×   2          ×   2          ×   2
 ─────          ─────          ─────
     8             68            468
```

Exercise

Find the products.

1.
```
  111
×   5
```

2.
```
  987
×   1
```

3.
```
  212
×   4
```

4.
```
  223
×   3
```

5.
```
  341
×   2
```

6.
```
  333
×   3
```

7.
```
  431
×   2
```

8.
```
  892
×   1
```

9.
```
  143
×   2
```

10.
```
  397
×   1
```

11.
```
  232
×   3
```

12.
```
  444
×   2
```

Multiplication

$3 \times 357 =$

Multiply ones.	Multiply tens.	Multiply hundreds.
3×7 ones $= 21$ ones Regroup. 21 ones is 2 tens and 1 one	3×5 tens $= 15$ tens Regroup. 15 tens is 1 hundred and 5 tens	3×3 hundreds $= 9$ hundreds Add them all up.

	hundreds	tens	ones
$\times$	3	5	7
			3
		2	1

	hundreds	tens	ones
$\times$	3	5	7
			3
		2	1
	1	5	

	hundreds	tens	ones
$\times$	3	5	7
			3
		2	1
	1	5	
	9		
	10	7	1

$3 \times 357 = 1071$

$835 \times 7 =$

Multiply ones.	Multiply tens.	Multiply hundreds.
7×5 ones $= 35$ ones Regroup. 35 ones is 3 tens and 5 ones	7×3 tens $= 21$ tens Regroup. 21 tens is 2 hundreds and 1 ten	7×8 hundreds $= 56$ hundreds 5 thousands and 6 hundreds Add them all up.

```
  835
×   7
─────
   35
```

```
  835
×   7
─────
   35
   21
```

```
  835
×   7
─────
   35
   21
   56
─────
 5845
```

$835 \times 7 = 5845$

Multiplication with Regrouping

Multiply:

$$\overset{1}{24}6$$
$$\times \quad 3$$
$$\overline{\quad\quad 8}$$

Multiply ones.
3 × 6 ones = 18 ones
Regroup.
18 ones is 1 ten and 8 ones

$$\overset{1\ 1}{24}6$$
$$\times \quad 3$$
$$\overline{\quad 38}$$

Multiply tens.
3 × 4 tens + 1 ten= 13 tens
Regroup.
13 tens is
1 hundreds and 3 tens

$$\overset{1\ 1}{24}6$$
$$\times \quad 3$$
$$\overline{738}$$

Multiply hundreds.
3 × 2 hundreds + 1 hundred
= 7 hundreds

246 × 3 = 738

Exercise

Find the products.

1. $\begin{array}{r}162\\ \times\ \ \ 4\\\hline\end{array}$	2. $\begin{array}{r}271\\ \times\ \ \ 2\\\hline\end{array}$	3. $\begin{array}{r}141\\ \times\ \ \ 6\\\hline\end{array}$	4. $\begin{array}{r}132\\ \times\ \ \ 7\\\hline\end{array}$
5. $\begin{array}{r}257\\ \times\ \ \ 3\\\hline\end{array}$	6. $\begin{array}{r}146\\ \times\ \ \ 7\\\hline\end{array}$	7. $\begin{array}{r}197\\ \times\ \ \ 4\\\hline\end{array}$	8. $\begin{array}{r}244\\ \times\ \ \ 3\\\hline\end{array}$
9. $\begin{array}{r}283\\ \times\ \ \ 2\\\hline\end{array}$	10. $\begin{array}{r}158\\ \times\ \ \ 5\\\hline\end{array}$	11. $\begin{array}{r}185\\ \times\ \ \ 4\\\hline\end{array}$	12. $\begin{array}{r}359\\ \times\ \ \ 2\\\hline\end{array}$
13. $\begin{array}{r}293\\ \times\ \ \ 6\\\hline\end{array}$	14. $\begin{array}{r}139\\ \times\ \ \ 6\\\hline\end{array}$	15. $\begin{array}{r}198\\ \times\ \ \ 3\\\hline\end{array}$	16. $\begin{array}{r}387\\ \times\ \ \ 5\\\hline\end{array}$

Exercise

Find the products.

1. 477
   × 2

2. 172
   × 5

3. 123
   × 7

4. 176
   × 4

5. 263
   × 3

6. 137
   × 5

7. 375
   × 2

8. 153
   × 4

9. 184
   × 3

10. 458
    × 2

11. 234
    × 4

12. 143
    × 5

13. 136
    × 6

14. 639
    × 5

15. 398
    × 7

16. 284
    × 3

17. 217
    × 8

18. 278
    × 4

19. 189
    × 5

20. 494
    × 3

21. If each of the 3 children picks 238 peaches, how many peaches will the 3 children have picked altogether?   _____

22. If John reads 153 pages a day, how many pages will he have read after 4 days?   _____

23. If each bus can hold 67 passengers, how many passengers can 5 buses hold?   _____

Multiplication

98

Multiplying Money

When multiplying money, follow the same rules for multiplying whole numbers.

Multiply:

$$\begin{array}{r} 5 \\ \$\,3.79 \\ \times \quad\ 6 \\ \hline 4 \end{array}$$

Multiply the pennies.
6 × 9 pennies = 54 pennies
Regroup. 54 pennies is 5 dimes and 4 pennies. Put the dimes at the top of the dimes place and the pennies in the pennies place.

$$\begin{array}{r} 4\ 5 \\ \$\,3.79 \\ \times \quad\ 6 \\ \hline 74 \end{array}$$

Multiply the dimes.
6 × 7 dimes + 5 dimes
= 47 dimes. Regroup.
47 dimes is 4 dollars and 7 dimes. Put the dollars at the top of the dollars place and the dimes in the dimes place.

$$\begin{array}{r} 4\ 5 \\ \$\,3.79 \\ \times \quad\ 6 \\ \hline 22\ 74 \end{array}$$

Multiply the dollars.
6 × 3 dollars + 4 dollars = 22 dollars.
Bring down the decimal point and write the $ sign.

$3.79 × 6 = $22.74

$$\begin{array}{r} 4\ 5 \\ \$\,3.79 \\ \times \quad\ 6 \\ \hline \$\,22.74 \end{array}$$

Exercise

Find the products.

1. $ 2.75
    ×   3

2. $ 3.89
    ×   2

3. $ 1.95
    ×   5

4. $ 1.69
    ×   4

5. $ 1.57
    ×   6

6. $ 2.48
    ×   3

7. $ 1.34
    ×   7

8. $ 2.58
    ×   3

Exercise

Find the products.

1. $ 2.70
   × 3

2. $ 3.02
   × 2

3. $ 1.28
   × 4

4. $ 1.93
   × 3

5. $ 1.60
   × 5

6. $ 1.63
   × 4

7. $ 2.47
   × 3

8. $ 6.45
   × 3

9. $ 4.57
   × 9

10. $ 3.87
    × 6

11. $ 4.81
    × 4

12. $ 8.32
    × 8

13. $ 2.39
    × 7

14. $ 2.79
    × 5

15. $ 7.23
    × 7

16. $ 9.72
    × 8

17. The box lunches cost $2.48 per box.
    How much will it take to buy 4 lunches?   _____

18. Ice cream cones are $1.46 apiece.
    If they bought 6, how much did they spend?   _____

19. How much would 7 corn dogs cost
    if each corn dog costs $1.28?   _____

20. The cotton candy was $1.63 and they
    bought 5 of them. How much did they pay?   _____

Objective #6 – Multiplication of Whole Numbers

The student will be able to multiply up to 4-digit whole numbers
by 1-digit numbers and will demonstrate his mastery by completing
the Skill Test for Objective #6 on pp. 198-199 quickly and accurately.

Multiplying Money

Exercise

Find the products.

1.
$$\begin{array}{r} 499 \\ \times\ \ 5 \\ \hline \end{array}$$

2.
$$\begin{array}{r} 712 \\ \times\ \ 6 \\ \hline \end{array}$$

3.
$$\begin{array}{r} 197 \\ \times\ \ 2 \\ \hline \end{array}$$

4.
$$\begin{array}{r} 149 \\ \times\ \ 3 \\ \hline \end{array}$$

5.
$$\begin{array}{r} 138 \\ \times\ \ 6 \\ \hline \end{array}$$

6.
$$\begin{array}{r} 278 \\ \times\ \ 4 \\ \hline \end{array}$$

7.
$$\begin{array}{r} 250 \\ \times\ \ 3 \\ \hline \end{array}$$

8.
$$\begin{array}{r} 273 \\ \times\ \ 8 \\ \hline \end{array}$$

9.
$$\begin{array}{r} 327 \\ \times\ \ 9 \\ \hline \end{array}$$

10.
$$\begin{array}{r} 297 \\ \times\ \ 6 \\ \hline \end{array}$$

11.
$$\begin{array}{r} 115 \\ \times\ \ 2 \\ \hline \end{array}$$

12.
$$\begin{array}{r} 957 \\ \times\ \ 6 \\ \hline \end{array}$$

13.
$$\begin{array}{r} 439 \\ \times\ \ 4 \\ \hline \end{array}$$

14.
$$\begin{array}{r} 689 \\ \times\ \ 8 \\ \hline \end{array}$$

15.
$$\begin{array}{r} 851 \\ \times\ \ 3 \\ \hline \end{array}$$

16.
$$\begin{array}{r} 575 \\ \times\ \ 4 \\ \hline \end{array}$$

17.
$$\begin{array}{r} \$1.71 \\ \times\ \ 8 \\ \hline \end{array}$$

18.
$$\begin{array}{r} \$5.39 \\ \times\ \ 4 \\ \hline \end{array}$$

19.
$$\begin{array}{r} \$7.05 \\ \times\ \ 5 \\ \hline \end{array}$$

20.
$$\begin{array}{r} \$6.21 \\ \times\ \ 8 \\ \hline \end{array}$$

21.
$$\begin{array}{r} \$2.76 \\ \times\ \ 2 \\ \hline \end{array}$$

22.
$$\begin{array}{r} \$7.31 \\ \times\ \ 9 \\ \hline \end{array}$$

23.
$$\begin{array}{r} \$1.89 \\ \times\ \ 7 \\ \hline \end{array}$$

24.
$$\begin{array}{r} \$4.66 \\ \times\ \ 3 \\ \hline \end{array}$$

25.
$$\begin{array}{r} \$8.96 \\ \times\ \ 6 \\ \hline \end{array}$$

26.
$$\begin{array}{r} \$5.83 \\ \times\ \ 4 \\ \hline \end{array}$$

27.
$$\begin{array}{r} \$3.29 \\ \times\ \ 5 \\ \hline \end{array}$$

28.
$$\begin{array}{r} \$6.38 \\ \times\ \ 8 \\ \hline \end{array}$$

29.
$$\begin{array}{r} \$6.75 \\ \times\ \ 8 \\ \hline \end{array}$$

30.
$$\begin{array}{r} \$5.93 \\ \times\ \ 6 \\ \hline \end{array}$$

31.
$$\begin{array}{r} \$3.48 \\ \times\ \ 9 \\ \hline \end{array}$$

32.
$$\begin{array}{r} \$9.89 \\ \times\ \ 4 \\ \hline \end{array}$$

Review

Exercise

Solve.

1. Each of the 3 fields has 645 plants in it.
    How many plants are in all 3 fields?   _____

2. Charles is paid $4.57 per hour doing yard work.
    If he works for 5 hours, how much will he make?   _____

3. Each bag contains 387 nuts.
    How many nuts are in 6 bags?   _____

4. If a gallon of gasoline costs $2.81,
    how much will 4 gallons cost?   _____

5. The round trip to Nashville and back
    is 832 miles. If you make the trip 8 times,
    how many miles will you travel?   _____

6. Mrs. Bennett paid $3.79 per pound
    for pistachios that were on sale. She
    bought 5 pounds. How much did she pay?   _____

7. Each lot contains 463 widgets.
    How many widgets are in 6 lots?   _____

8. The rental rate for the scooter was
    $9.10 per hour. If the scooter was rented
    for 2 hours, what would be the cost?   _____

If you have not already done so, complete the Skills Test for Objective #6 on pp. 198-199. When you have successfully completed the test you may check it off on your objectives list on page 186.

Review

Division

Before we begin learning more about division, let's take a moment and review our basic division facts, because we will need to know them very well if we are to be successful in this chapter.

Divide:

1. $20 \div 4 =$ _____
2. $8\overline{)64}$
3. $20 \div 5 =$ _____
4. $6\overline{)36}$

5. $72 \div 8 =$ _____
6. $6\overline{)30}$
7. $72 \div 9 =$ _____
8. $6\overline{)42}$

9. $48 \div 8 =$ _____
10. $6\overline{)24}$
11. $35 \div 7 =$ _____
12. $7\overline{)42}$

13. $21 \div 3 =$ _____
14. $7\overline{)56}$
15. $28 \div 7 =$ _____
16. $4\overline{)24}$

17. $40 \div 5 =$ _____
18. $9\overline{)63}$
19. $21 \div 7 =$ _____
20. $8\overline{)24}$

21. $32 \div 4 =$ _____
22. $5\overline{)25}$
23. $48 \div 6 =$ _____
24. $7\overline{)49}$

25. $35 \div 5 =$ _____
26. $6\overline{)54}$
27. $18 \div 2 =$ _____
28. $5\overline{)30}$

29. $15 \div 3 =$ _____
30. $6\overline{)42}$
31. $40 \div 8 =$ _____
32. $8\overline{)56}$

33. $18 \div 9 =$ _____
34. $3\overline{)24}$
35. $15 \div 5 =$ _____
36. $9\overline{)54}$

37. $12 \div 4 =$ _____
38. $7\overline{)63}$
39. $32 \div 8 =$ _____
40. $3\overline{)9}$

41. $28 \div 4 =$ _____
42. $4\overline{)16}$
43. $12 \div 3 =$ _____
44. $9\overline{)81}$

Division

We are going to learn how to divide 2 and 3-digit dividends by a 1-digit divisor. Let's look at an example:

We ask ourselves what we can multiply by 8 that will be close to but not more than 35.

$$8 \overline{)35}$$

□ × 8 = 35	4 × 8 = 32

We write:

$$\begin{array}{r} 4 \\ 8\overline{)35} \\ \underline{32} \\ 3 \end{array}$$

Then subtract:

So we say: 8 goes into 35
4 times with 3 left over.
We write the quotient like this:

4 R 3

which is read as: 4 remainder 3

Let's try another: 20 ÷ 6 = _____

Follow these steps:

❶ Estimate

$$\begin{array}{r} 3 \\ 6\overline{)20} \end{array}$$

6 will go into 20
about 3 times

❷ Multiply

$$\begin{array}{r} 3 \\ 6\overline{)20} \\ 18 \end{array}$$

6 × 3 = 18

❸ Subtract

$$\begin{array}{r} 3 \\ 6\overline{)20} \\ \underline{18} \\ 2 \end{array}$$

20 − 18 = 2

If the remainder is larger than the divisor, then repeat steps 1 – 3.
If smaller than the divisor, write the remainder with the quotient.   3 R 2
If zero, there is no remainder.

Try These

1. $4\overline{)26}$ 2. $3\overline{)19}$ 3. $5\overline{)27}$ 4. $7\overline{)25}$

Division

Let's review our terms:

$$\begin{array}{r} 16 \\ 4{\overline{)64}} \end{array}$$

divisor → quotient, dividend

$$64 \div 4 = 16$$

dividend → quotient ← divisor

Divide. Follow the steps. $64 \div 4$

❶ Estimate

$$\begin{array}{r} 10 \\ 4{\overline{)64}} \end{array}$$

4 will go into 6
1 time

❷ Multiply

$$\begin{array}{r} 10 \\ 4{\overline{)64}} \\ 40 \end{array}$$

$4 \times 10 = 40$

❸ Subtract

$$\begin{array}{r} 10 \\ 4{\overline{)64}} \\ 40 \\ \hline 24 \end{array}$$

$64 - 40 = 24$

If the remainder is larger than the divisor, then repeat steps 1 – 3.
If smaller than the divisor, write the remainder with the quotient.
If zero, there is no remainder.

❶ Estimate

$$\begin{array}{r} 1 \\ 4{\overline{)64}} \\ 40 \\ \hline 24 \end{array}$$

4 will go into 24
about 6 times

❷ Multiply

$$\begin{array}{r} 16 \\ 4{\overline{)64}} \\ 40 \\ \hline 24 \\ 24 \end{array}$$

$4 \times 6 = 24$

❸ Subtract

$$\begin{array}{r} 16 \\ 4{\overline{)64}} \\ 40 \\ \hline 24 \\ 24 \\ \hline 0 \end{array}$$

$24 - 24 = 0$

If the remainder is larger than the divisor, then repeat steps 1 – 3.
If smaller than the divisor, write the remainder with the quotient.

$64 \div 4 = 16$ If zero, there is no remainder.

Try These (continued)

5. $4{\overline{)15}}$ 6. $7{\overline{)45}}$ 7. $8{\overline{)20}}$ 8. $6{\overline{)35}}$

9. $4{\overline{)30}}$ 10. $9{\overline{)50}}$ 11. $5{\overline{)43}}$ 12. $3{\overline{)25}}$

Divide. Follow the steps.

1. $5\overline{)32}$

2. $3\overline{)14}$

3. $9\overline{)29}$

4. $7\overline{)17}$

5. $6\overline{)56}$

6. $3\overline{)10}$

7. $8\overline{)50}$

8. $7\overline{)32}$

9. $2\overline{)59}$

10. $2\overline{)25}$

11. $5\overline{)87}$

12. $4\overline{)97}$

13. $2\overline{)48}$

14. $3\overline{)69}$

15. $4\overline{)62}$

16. $8\overline{)88}$

17. $5\overline{)65}$

18. $6\overline{)84}$

19. $7\overline{)91}$

20. $6\overline{)77}$

Objective #7 – Division of Whole Numbers

The student will be able to divide 2- and 3-digit dividends by 1-digit divisors resulting in 1-, 2-, or 3-digit quotients with and without remainders and will demonstrate his mastery by completing the Skill Test for Objective #7 on pp. 200-201 quickly and accurately.

Division

Solve.

1. Mother taught Anne and Mary how to bake
    cookies today. They baked 20 cookies, to be
    given to the family for dessert. If each person
    had 2 cookies, how many family members were there?   _____

2. Father took the boys out for a tennis lesson
    as their homeschool physical activity of the day.
    If he brought 24 balls, and there were 3 in each can,
    how many cans did he bring?   _____

3. The Delaney children dyed Easter eggs on Holy
    Saturday. If there were 20 eggs and 5 children,
    how many did each child have to decorate?   _____

4. The Seton Knights averaged 5 points per softball
    game. At this rate, how many games would it take
    them to have a total of 30 points?   _____

5. Jane solved a total of 72 math problems over 9 days.
    How many would this equal per day?   _____

6. Sean is helping his mother plant a vegetable garden.
    How many rows will he plant if he plants 6 seeds in
    each row and he has 75 seeds? Will there be any left
    over? How many?   _____

7. Joseph has 84 holy cards. If he puts up the
    same number of cards on each of 4 walls,
    how many holy cards are on each wall?   _____

8. Maria has 94 stamps in her collection.
    She puts the same number of stamps on each
    of the 8 pages in her stamp book with some left
    over. At most, how many stamps could be on each
    page and how many would be left over?   _____

9. There are 4 cups in 1 quart. If I have
    82 cups, how many quarts do I have?
    How many cups are left over?   _____

Checking Division

To check division, we multiply the divisor by the quotient and then add any remainder. The sum should be the same as the dividend.

```
quotient ↘ 23 R 2 ↙ remainder          quotient ↘ 23
         4)94 ↖                                  ×   4  ← divisor
divisor ↗   80  ↖ dividend                      ───
          ───                                    92
           14                                  +   2  ← remainder
           12                                  ───
          ───              dividend → 94
            2
```

Exercise

Divide and check.

	check		check		check
1. 4)97		2. 3)54		3. 5)85	
4. 8)98		5. 4)69		6. 3)83	
7. 2)48		8. 3)93		9. 5)55	
10. 4)92		11. 8)70		12. 5)18	

3-Digit Dividends

The terms and the steps are the same when using a 3-digit dividend.

quotient $\searrow$ $\nearrow$ remainder
$$41 \text{ R } 1$$
divisor $\nearrow$ $4\overline{)165}$
$\nwarrow$ dividend

dividend $\nearrow$ $165 \div 4 = 41 \text{ R } 1$ $\swarrow$ quotient
$\nwarrow$ divisor

Example: $165 \div 4$ Divide. Follow the steps.

❶ Estimate

$$\begin{array}{r} 40 \\ 4\overline{)165} \end{array}$$

4 will go into 16
4 times

❷ Multiply

$$\begin{array}{r} 40 \\ 4\overline{)165} \\ 160 \end{array}$$

$4 \times 40 = 160$

❸ Subtract

$$\begin{array}{r} 40 \\ 4\overline{)165} \\ \underline{160} \\ 5 \end{array}$$

$165 - 160 = 5$

If the remainder is larger than the divisor, then repeat steps 1 – 3.
If smaller than the divisor, write the remainder with the quotient.
If zero, there is no remainder.

❶ Estimate

$$\begin{array}{r} 40 \\ 4\overline{)165} \\ \underline{160} \\ 5 \end{array}$$

4 will go into 5
1 time

❷ Multiply

$$\begin{array}{r} 41 \\ 4\overline{)165} \\ 160 \\ 5 \\ 4 \end{array}$$

$4 \times 1 = 4$

❸ Subtract

$$\begin{array}{r} 41 \\ 4\overline{)165} \\ 160 \\ 5 \\ \underline{4} \\ 1 \end{array}$$

$5 - 4 = 1$

If the remainder is larger than the divisor, then repeat 1 – 3.
If not then write the remainder with the quotient. $165 \div 4 = 41 \text{ R } 1$

Try These

1. $4\overline{)244}$

2. $3\overline{)186}$

3. $5\overline{)273}$

4. $7\overline{)245}$

Exercise

Divide. Follow the steps.

1. $4\overline{)264}$
2. $3\overline{)198}$
3. $5\overline{)252}$
4. $7\overline{)284}$

5. $8\overline{)325}$
6. $9\overline{)549}$
7. $2\overline{)144}$
8. $5\overline{)392}$

9. $7\overline{)658}$
10. $6\overline{)492}$
11. $4\overline{)248}$
12. $3\overline{)291}$

13. $2\overline{)64}$
14. $4\overline{)372}$
15. $6\overline{)547}$
16. $8\overline{)428}$

17. $5\overline{)197}$
18. $6\overline{)426}$
19. $3\overline{)165}$
20. $2\overline{)42}$

Dividing Money

When dividing money, use the same terms and steps as when dividing whole numbers, then bring up the decimal and write the $ sign.

quotient → $.65
divisor → 8)$5.20
dividend ↗

quotient ↙
dividend ↗ $5.20 ÷ 8 = $.65 ← divisor

Example: $5.20 ÷ 8 Divide. Follow the steps.

❶ Estimate

60
8)$5.20

8 will go into 52
6 times

❷ Multiply

60
8)$5.20
4 80

8 × 60 = 480

❸ Subtract

60
8)$5.20
4 80
40

520 – 480 = 40

If the remainder is larger than the divisor, then repeat steps 1 – 3.
If smaller than the divisor, write the remainder with the quotient.
If zero, there is no remainder.

❶ Estimate

6
8)$5.20
4 80
40

8 will go into 40
5 times

❷ Multiply

65
8)$5.20
4 80
40
40

8 × 5 = 40

❸ Subtract

$ .65
8)$5.20
4 80
40
40
0

40 – 40 = 0

If the remainder is larger than the divisor, then repeat 1 – 3.
If not then bring up the decimal and write the $ sign. $5.20 ÷ 8 = $.65

Try These

1. $.
   7)$2.66

2. $.
   5)$1.90

3. $.
   9)$2.79

4. $.
   6)$2.58

If you have not already done so, complete the Skills Test for Objective #7 on pp. 200-201. When you have successfully completed the test you may check it off on your objectives list on page 186.

Dividing Money

Review

Divide. Follow the steps. Use $ signs and decimals when necessary.

1. $6\overline{)81}$

2. $6\overline{)77}$

3. $4\overline{)65}$

4. $3\overline{)71}$

5. $9\overline{)91}$

6. $3\overline{)79}$

7. $7\overline{)90}$

8. $5\overline{)83}$

9. $5\overline{)415}$

10. $4\overline{)148}$

11. $7\overline{)539}$

12. $6\overline{)504}$

13. $7\overline{)444}$

14. $6\overline{)534}$

15. $8\overline{)492}$

16. $9\overline{)401}$

17. $4\overline{)\$3.44}$

18. $4\overline{)\$2.48}$

19. $3\overline{)\$2.49}$

20. $8\overline{)\$4.24}$

Review

Fractions

A fraction is a part of a whole.
It can also be a part of a set.

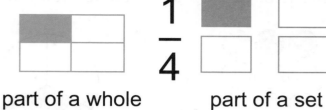

part of a whole   part of a set

number of equal parts shaded ➲   **3**   ↶ numerator

total number of equal parts

in the whole or in the set ➲   **4**   ↶ denominator

$$\frac{3}{4}$$

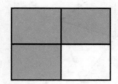   or   Say: three fourths

Try These

Write the fraction for each shaded part.

1.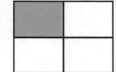

_____

2.

_____

3.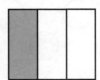

_____

4.

_____

5.

_____

6.

_____

7.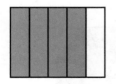

_____

113

Exercise

Write the fraction for each shaded part of a whole or a set.

1.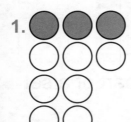

_____

2.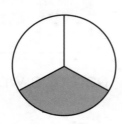

_____

3.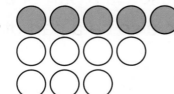

_____

4.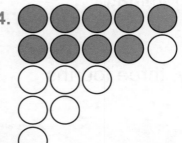

_____

5.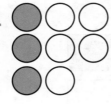

_____

6.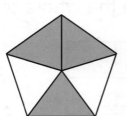

_____

7.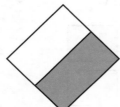

_____

8.

_____

9.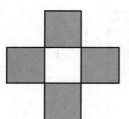

_____

10.

_____

11.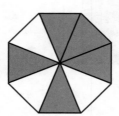

_____

12.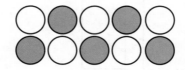

_____

13.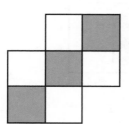

_____

Exercise

Write each as a fraction.

1. one fourth _____

2. one third _____

3. one half _____

4. three tenths _____

5. two thirds _____

6. one sixth _____

7. five eighths _____

8. two sevenths _____

9. two thirds _____

10. three fourths _____

11. seven eighths _____

12. one fifth _____

13. five tenths _____

14. one twelfth _____

15. nine tenths _____

Write the word name for each fraction.

16. $\frac{1}{4}$ _____

17. $\frac{3}{4}$ _____

18. $\frac{2}{5}$ _____

19. $\frac{4}{5}$ _____

20. $\frac{2}{3}$ _____

21. $\frac{1}{3}$ _____

22. $\frac{3}{5}$ _____

23. $\frac{1}{6}$ _____

24. $\frac{1}{8}$ _____

25. $\frac{1}{10}$ _____

Exercise

Draw a picture to show each fraction.

1. $\dfrac{1}{2}$

2. $\dfrac{1}{3}$

3. $\dfrac{1}{5}$

4. $\dfrac{4}{5}$

5. $\dfrac{1}{4}$

6. $\dfrac{1}{8}$

7. $\dfrac{3}{10}$

8. $\dfrac{3}{6}$

9. $\dfrac{5}{10}$

10. $\dfrac{1}{10}$

Equivalent Fractions

A fraction can name one or more equal parts of a whole or of a set.

Different fractions can name the same amount.

Fractions that name the same amount are called **equivalent fractions**.

When we studied division we learned that:

> **When you divide a number by itself, the quotient is 1.**

It is the same way with fractions:

$$1 = \tfrac{2}{2} = \tfrac{3}{3} = \tfrac{4}{4} = \tfrac{5}{5} = \tfrac{6}{6} = \tfrac{7}{7} = \tfrac{8}{8} = \tfrac{9}{9} = \tfrac{10}{10} = \tfrac{12}{12} = \tfrac{16}{16}$$

> **When the numerator and the denominator are the same the fraction is equal to one.**

That is one example of equivalent fractions. Look at the fraction table and see if you can find some other examples.

Look at the $\tfrac{1}{2}$

How many $\tfrac{1}{4}$s are there in $\tfrac{1}{2}$?

Fraction Table

$$1 = \tfrac{2}{2} = \tfrac{3}{3} = \tfrac{4}{4} = \tfrac{5}{5} = \tfrac{6}{6} = \tfrac{7}{7} = \tfrac{8}{8} = \tfrac{9}{9} = \tfrac{10}{10} = \tfrac{12}{12} = \tfrac{16}{16}$$

Try These

Write as many equivalent fractions for each of the following as you can:

1. $\dfrac{1}{2}$

   _____

2. $\dfrac{1}{4}$ 3. $\dfrac{4}{12}$ 4. $\dfrac{12}{16}$

   _____   _____   _____

5. $\dfrac{1}{5}$ 6. $\dfrac{4}{6}$ 7. $\dfrac{6}{8}$

   _____   _____   _____

117

Equivalent Fractions

Fractions that are equal are called **equivalent fractions**.
Equivalent fractions name the same amount.

On the next page you find fractions strips that you may use to help you understand equivalent fractions. You may cut each of the fraction strips into equal parts and put the pieces from each in a different pile.

Place a fraction piece for ½ in your work area. Using the pieces that show fourths,

determine how many pieces equal ½.

$\frac{1}{2}$	
$\frac{1}{4}$	$\frac{1}{4}$

Try These

Shade the second figure so that it is equal to the first figure. Then complete.

1.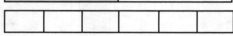

$$\frac{1}{2} = \frac{?}{6}$$
_____

2.

$$\frac{1}{4} = \frac{?}{8}$$
_____

3.

$$\frac{2}{3} = \frac{?}{12}$$
_____

4.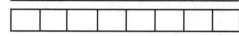

$$\frac{2}{4} = \frac{?}{16}$$
_____

5.

$$\frac{1}{3} = \frac{?}{15}$$
_____

6.

$$\frac{2}{5} = \frac{?}{10}$$
_____

7.

$$\frac{2}{6} = \frac{?}{12}$$
_____

8.

$$\frac{5}{5} = \frac{?}{10}$$
_____

| $\frac{1}{2}$ | | $\frac{1}{2}$ | |

| $\frac{1}{4}$ | $\frac{1}{4}$ | $\frac{1}{4}$ | $\frac{1}{4}$ |

| $\frac{1}{6}$ | $\frac{1}{6}$ | $\frac{1}{6}$ | $\frac{1}{6}$ | $\frac{1}{6}$ | $\frac{1}{6}$ |

| $\frac{1}{8}$ | $\frac{1}{8}$ | $\frac{1}{8}$ | $\frac{1}{8}$ | $\frac{1}{8}$ | $\frac{1}{8}$ | $\frac{1}{8}$ | $\frac{1}{8}$ |

| $\frac{1}{10}$ | $\frac{1}{10}$ | $\frac{1}{10}$ | $\frac{1}{10}$ | $\frac{1}{10}$ | $\frac{1}{10}$ | $\frac{1}{10}$ | $\frac{1}{10}$ | $\frac{1}{10}$ | $\frac{1}{10}$ |

| $\frac{1}{12}$ | $\frac{1}{12}$ | $\frac{1}{12}$ | $\frac{1}{12}$ | $\frac{1}{12}$ | $\frac{1}{12}$ | $\frac{1}{12}$ | $\frac{1}{12}$ | $\frac{1}{12}$ | $\frac{1}{12}$ | $\frac{1}{12}$ | $\frac{1}{12}$ |

| $\frac{1}{16}$ | $\frac{1}{16}$ | $\frac{1}{16}$ | $\frac{1}{16}$ | $\frac{1}{16}$ | $\frac{1}{16}$ | $\frac{1}{16}$ | $\frac{1}{16}$ | $\frac{1}{16}$ | $\frac{1}{16}$ | $\frac{1}{16}$ | $\frac{1}{16}$ | $\frac{1}{16}$ | $\frac{1}{16}$ | $\frac{1}{16}$ | $\frac{1}{16}$ |

| $\frac{1}{3}$ | | $\frac{1}{3}$ | | $\frac{1}{3}$ | |

| $\frac{1}{5}$ | $\frac{1}{5}$ | $\frac{1}{5}$ | $\frac{1}{5}$ | $\frac{1}{5}$ |

| $\frac{1}{6}$ | $\frac{1}{6}$ | $\frac{1}{6}$ | $\frac{1}{6}$ | $\frac{1}{6}$ | $\frac{1}{6}$ |

| $\frac{1}{9}$ | $\frac{1}{9}$ | $\frac{1}{9}$ | $\frac{1}{9}$ | $\frac{1}{9}$ | $\frac{1}{9}$ | $\frac{1}{9}$ | $\frac{1}{9}$ | $\frac{1}{9}$ |

| $\frac{1}{10}$ | $\frac{1}{10}$ | $\frac{1}{10}$ | $\frac{1}{10}$ | $\frac{1}{10}$ | $\frac{1}{10}$ | $\frac{1}{10}$ | $\frac{1}{10}$ | $\frac{1}{10}$ | $\frac{1}{10}$ |

| $\frac{1}{15}$ | $\frac{1}{15}$ | $\frac{1}{15}$ | $\frac{1}{15}$ | $\frac{1}{15}$ | $\frac{1}{15}$ | $\frac{1}{15}$ | $\frac{1}{15}$ | $\frac{1}{15}$ | $\frac{1}{15}$ | $\frac{1}{15}$ | $\frac{1}{15}$ | $\frac{1}{15}$ | $\frac{1}{15}$ | $\frac{1}{15}$ |

$\frac{1}{2}$	$\frac{1}{2}$

$\frac{1}{4}$	$\frac{1}{4}$	$\frac{1}{4}$	$\frac{1}{4}$

$\frac{1}{6}$	$\frac{1}{6}$	$\frac{1}{6}$	$\frac{1}{6}$	$\frac{1}{6}$	$\frac{1}{6}$

$\frac{1}{8}$	$\frac{1}{8}$	$\frac{1}{8}$	$\frac{1}{8}$	$\frac{1}{8}$	$\frac{1}{8}$	$\frac{1}{8}$	$\frac{1}{8}$

$\frac{1}{10}$	$\frac{1}{10}$	$\frac{1}{10}$	$\frac{1}{10}$	$\frac{1}{10}$	$\frac{1}{10}$	$\frac{1}{10}$	$\frac{1}{10}$	$\frac{1}{10}$	$\frac{1}{10}$

$\frac{1}{12}$	$\frac{1}{12}$	$\frac{1}{12}$	$\frac{1}{12}$	$\frac{1}{12}$	$\frac{1}{12}$	$\frac{1}{12}$	$\frac{1}{12}$	$\frac{1}{12}$	$\frac{1}{12}$	$\frac{1}{12}$	$\frac{1}{12}$

$\frac{1}{16}$	$\frac{1}{16}$	$\frac{1}{16}$	$\frac{1}{16}$	$\frac{1}{16}$	$\frac{1}{16}$	$\frac{1}{16}$	$\frac{1}{16}$	$\frac{1}{16}$	$\frac{1}{16}$	$\frac{1}{16}$	$\frac{1}{16}$	$\frac{1}{16}$	$\frac{1}{16}$	$\frac{1}{16}$	$\frac{1}{16}$

When you divide a number by itself, the quotient is 1.

When multiplying, if one of the factors is one, then the product is the other factor.

When the numerator and the denominator are the same the fraction is equal to one.

When multiplying fractions, if one of the fractions is equal to one, then the product is the other fraction.

$\frac{1}{3}$	$\frac{1}{3}$	$\frac{1}{3}$

$\frac{1}{5}$	$\frac{1}{5}$	$\frac{1}{5}$	$\frac{1}{5}$	$\frac{1}{5}$

$\frac{1}{6}$	$\frac{1}{6}$	$\frac{1}{6}$	$\frac{1}{6}$	$\frac{1}{6}$	$\frac{1}{6}$

$\frac{1}{9}$	$\frac{1}{9}$	$\frac{1}{9}$	$\frac{1}{9}$	$\frac{1}{9}$	$\frac{1}{9}$	$\frac{1}{9}$	$\frac{1}{9}$	$\frac{1}{9}$

$\frac{1}{10}$	$\frac{1}{10}$	$\frac{1}{10}$	$\frac{1}{10}$	$\frac{1}{10}$	$\frac{1}{10}$	$\frac{1}{10}$	$\frac{1}{10}$	$\frac{1}{10}$	$\frac{1}{10}$

$\frac{1}{15}$	$\frac{1}{15}$	$\frac{1}{15}$	$\frac{1}{15}$	$\frac{1}{15}$	$\frac{1}{15}$	$\frac{1}{15}$	$\frac{1}{15}$	$\frac{1}{15}$	$\frac{1}{15}$	$\frac{1}{15}$	$\frac{1}{15}$	$\frac{1}{15}$	$\frac{1}{15}$	$\frac{1}{15}$

Exercise

Write the equivalent fraction for each. You may use the fraction strips.

1. $\dfrac{1}{6} = \dfrac{?}{12}$ _____

2. $\dfrac{3}{5} = \dfrac{?}{10}$ _____

3. $\dfrac{1}{3} = \dfrac{?}{9}$ _____

4. $\dfrac{4}{16} = \dfrac{?}{4}$ _____

5. $\dfrac{2}{4} = \dfrac{?}{8}$ _____

6. $\dfrac{3}{6} = \dfrac{?}{12}$ _____

7. $\dfrac{1}{3} = \dfrac{?}{6}$ _____

8. $\dfrac{1}{4} = \dfrac{?}{8}$ _____

9. $\dfrac{2}{6} = \dfrac{?}{3}$ _____

10. $\dfrac{2}{5} = \dfrac{?}{10}$ _____

11. $\dfrac{3}{4} = \dfrac{?}{8}$ _____

12. $\dfrac{4}{8} = \dfrac{?}{4}$ _____

13. $\dfrac{2}{10} = \dfrac{?}{5}$ _____

14. $\dfrac{8}{10} = \dfrac{?}{5}$ _____

15. $\dfrac{4}{8} = \dfrac{?}{2}$ _____

16. $\dfrac{3}{4} = \dfrac{?}{12}$ _____

17. $\dfrac{10}{12} = \dfrac{?}{6}$ _____

18. $\dfrac{6}{10} = \dfrac{?}{5}$ _____

19. $\dfrac{4}{6} = \dfrac{?}{3}$ _____

20. $\dfrac{5}{10} = \dfrac{?}{2}$ _____

Equivalent Fractions

Different fractions can name the same amount.

> **When you divide a number by itself, the quotient is 1.**

> **When multiplying, if one of the factors is one, then the product is the other factor.**

> **When the numerator and the denominator are the same the fraction is equal to one.**

> **When multiplying fractions, if one of the fractions is equal to one, then the product is the other fraction.**

Fractions that name the same amount are called **equivalent fractions**.

$$1 = \frac{2}{2} = \frac{3}{3} = \frac{4}{4} = \frac{5}{5} = \frac{6}{6} = \frac{7}{7} = \frac{8}{8} = \frac{9}{9} = \frac{10}{10} = \frac{12}{12} = \frac{16}{16}$$

We can find equivalent fractions by multiplying by one in different ways.

Example: Find some equivalent fractions for $\frac{1}{4}$ by multiplying by one.

$$\frac{1}{4} \times \frac{2}{2} = \frac{2}{8} \qquad \frac{1}{4} \times \frac{3}{3} = \frac{3}{12} \qquad \frac{1}{4} \times \frac{4}{4} = \frac{4}{16} \qquad \frac{1}{4} \times \frac{5}{5} = \frac{5}{20}$$

Try These

Multiply each fraction by a form of one to determine an equivalent fraction.

1. $\frac{1}{3} \times = $ _____

2. $\frac{2}{5} \times = $ _____

3. $\frac{3}{6} \times = $ _____

4. $\frac{1}{2} \times = $ _____

5. $\frac{1}{6} \times = $ _____

6. $\frac{4}{5} \times = $ _____

7. $\frac{1}{5} \times = $ _____

8. $\frac{2}{3} \times = $ _____

9. $\frac{3}{4} \times = $ _____

Comparing Fractions

When two fractions have the same denominator then compare the numerator.

Example: Compare: $\frac{1}{3}$ 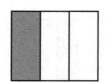 $\frac{2}{3}$

The denominators are the same.
Compare the numerators. 1< 2

$$\frac{1}{3} \; < \; \frac{2}{3}$$

Try These

Compare:

1. $\frac{2}{5} \bigcirc \frac{3}{5}$ 2. $\frac{1}{4} \bigcirc \frac{3}{4}$ 3. $\frac{1}{2} \bigcirc \frac{2}{2}$

4. $\frac{1}{3} \bigcirc \frac{2}{3}$ 5. $\frac{5}{6} \bigcirc \frac{4}{6}$ 6. $\frac{3}{7} \bigcirc \frac{4}{7}$

7. $\frac{8}{9} \bigcirc \frac{3}{9}$ 8. $\frac{3}{8} \bigcirc \frac{5}{8}$ 9. $\frac{6}{7} \bigcirc \frac{3}{7}$

10. $\frac{2}{4} \bigcirc \frac{1}{4}$ 11. $\frac{3}{6} \bigcirc \frac{5}{6}$ 12. $\frac{2}{8} \bigcirc \frac{7}{8}$

13. $\frac{2}{3} \bigcirc \frac{1}{3}$ 14. $\frac{3}{4} \bigcirc \frac{1}{4}$ 15. $\frac{2}{3} \bigcirc \frac{3}{3}$

16. $\frac{4}{10} \bigcirc \frac{7}{10}$ 17. $\frac{3}{9} \bigcirc \frac{1}{9}$ 18. $\frac{4}{12} \bigcirc \frac{8}{12}$

19. $\frac{1}{16} \bigcirc \frac{2}{16}$ 20. $\frac{5}{7} \bigcirc \frac{2}{7}$ 21. $\frac{1}{10} \bigcirc \frac{5}{10}$

Comparing Fractions

When two fractions do not have the same denominator then use fraction strips.

Example: Compare: $\dfrac{1}{4}$? $\dfrac{2}{3}$

The denominators are not the same.
Compare with fraction strips.
Which shows more?

$\dfrac{1}{4}$ < $\dfrac{2}{3}$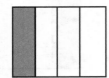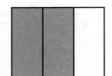

Try These

Compare:

1.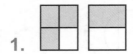

$\dfrac{3}{4}$ ◯ $\dfrac{1}{2}$

2.

$\dfrac{4}{5}$ ◯ $\dfrac{8}{10}$

3.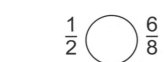

$\dfrac{1}{2}$ ◯ $\dfrac{6}{8}$

4.

$\dfrac{1}{2}$ ◯ $\dfrac{1}{4}$

5.

$\dfrac{1}{2}$ ◯ $\dfrac{1}{3}$

6.

$\dfrac{3}{8}$ ◯ $\dfrac{3}{4}$

7.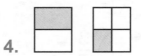

$\dfrac{2}{5}$ ◯ $\dfrac{2}{6}$

8.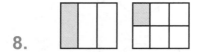

$\dfrac{1}{3}$ ◯ $\dfrac{1}{6}$

9.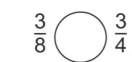

$\dfrac{1}{2}$ ◯ $\dfrac{5}{8}$

10.

$\dfrac{3}{4}$ ◯ $\dfrac{2}{5}$

11.

$\dfrac{2}{3}$ ◯ $\dfrac{4}{6}$

12.

$\dfrac{1}{2}$ ◯ $\dfrac{6}{10}$

Finding One Part of a Number

Find $\frac{1}{4}$ of **8.**   The numerator is 1 and the denominator shows the total number of equal parts. When the numerator is 1, we simply divide the number by the denominator.

$\frac{1}{4}$ of 8   Since the numerator is 1 we just divide by the denominator, which is **4.**   8 ÷ 4 = 2

So: $\frac{1}{4}$ of 8 = 2

Look at these examples:

$\frac{1}{2}$ of 10 = 10 ÷ 2 = 5 $\frac{1}{3}$ of 9 = 9 ÷ 3 = 3

$\frac{1}{2}$ of 8 = 8 ÷ 2 = 4 $\frac{1}{5}$ of 45 = 45 ÷ 5 = 9

Try These

Find one part of a number.

1. $\frac{1}{3}$ of 12 = 12 ÷ 3 = _____   2. $\frac{1}{2}$ of 8 = 8 ÷ 2 = _____

3. $\frac{1}{3}$ of 15 = 15 ÷ 3 = _____   4. $\frac{1}{4}$ of 32 = 32 ÷ 4 = _____

5. $\frac{1}{3}$ of 27   6. $\frac{1}{4}$ of 20   7. $\frac{1}{5}$ of 25

_____   _____   _____

8. $\frac{1}{4}$ of 16   9. $\frac{1}{2}$ of 10   10. $\frac{1}{4}$ of 28

_____   _____   _____

11. $\frac{1}{7}$ of 21   12. $\frac{1}{5}$ of 45   13. $\frac{1}{6}$ of 18

_____   _____   _____

Finding a Fraction of a Number

If we are finding more than one part of a number we must first multiply the number by the numerator before we divide by the denominator.

For example, if we wanted to find $\frac{2}{3}$ of 9, we would first have to multiply by 2 and then divide the product of 18 by **3.**

Find $\frac{2}{3}$ of 9   First multiply the 9 by the numerator of **2.** $9 \times 2 = 18$
$\frac{2}{3}$ of 9 = 6   Next, divide the product by the denominator. $18 \div 3 = 6$

Another method:

Find $\frac{2}{3}$ of 9   First find one part of the number as on the previous page. Divide the number by the denominator. $9 \div 3 = 3$
Then multiply by the numerator. $3 \times 2 = 6$

$\frac{2}{3}$ of 9 = 6   You may use either method:

Look at these examples:

$\frac{3}{5}$ of 10 = $10 \times 3 = 30$ $\frac{2}{3}$ of 12 = $12 \div 3 = 4$
             $30 \div 5 = 6$ $4 \times 2 = 8$
$\frac{3}{5}$ of 10 = 6 $\frac{2}{3}$ of 12 = 8

Try These

Find the fraction of a number. Use either method.

1. $\frac{2}{5}$ of 15 =   2. $\frac{2}{3}$ of 24 =

    _____   _____

3. $\frac{3}{5}$ of 25 =   4. $\frac{3}{4}$ of 32 =

    _____   _____

Exercise

Solve.

1. The Furtado family has 10 children and $\frac{1}{2}$ of them are boys? How many are boys?

   _____

2. The Bennetts have 12 children and $\frac{1}{4}$ of them are girls? How many are girls?

   _____

3. There were 24 candles by the St. Joseph statue at church and $\frac{1}{3}$ of them were lit. How many were lit?

   _____

4. Joseph decided to give $\frac{1}{5}$ of his holy card collection to his little sister for her birthday. How many will he give her if his collection has 95 cards in it?

   _____

5. Dad has 72 jellybeans. He put $\frac{1}{6}$ of them in each basket. How many are in each basket?

   _____

6. There were 25 questions on the test. If Martha got $\frac{4}{5}$ of them right, how many did she get right?

   _____

7. Mike scored $\frac{2}{3}$ of the 60 points the team scored. How many points did he score?

   _____

8. Of the 40 people crowded onto the small bus, $\frac{1}{8}$ could not find seats. How many people could not find seats?

   _____

9. Three fourths of the 32 students raised their hands to volunteer. How many raised their hands?

   _____

Objective #8 – Fractions

The student will be able to find a fractional part of a number and be able to add and subtract simple fractions with common denominators and will demonstrate his mastery by completing the Skill Test for Objective #8 on p. 202 quickly and accurately.

A mixed number is a number made up of a whole number and a fraction.

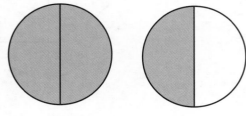

$1\frac{1}{2}$

$\frac{2}{2}$ = 1 whole $\quad$ $\frac{1}{2}$

$1\frac{1}{2}$

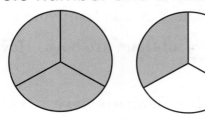

$1\frac{1}{3}$

$\frac{3}{3}$ = 1 whole $\quad$ $\frac{1}{3}$

$1\frac{1}{3}$

Try These

Write the mixed number for each.

1. 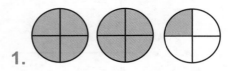 _____

2. 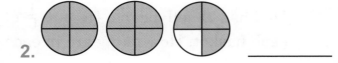 _____

3. 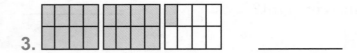 _____

4. 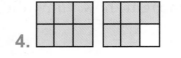 _____

5. 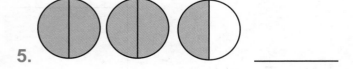 _____

6. 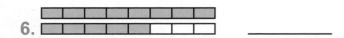 _____

7.  _____

8. 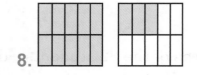 _____

9. 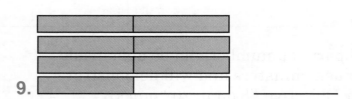 _____

10. 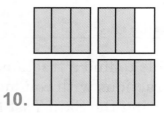 _____

Mixed Numbers

Adding Fractions

When the denominators are the same, we only add the numerators. The denominator remains the same.

$$\frac{1}{3} + \frac{1}{3} = \frac{2}{3}$$

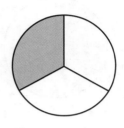 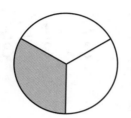

$$\frac{1}{5} + \frac{2}{5} = \frac{3}{5}$$

Try These

Shade each drawing to find the sum then write the sum.

1. | $\frac{1}{4}$ | $\frac{1}{4}$ | $\frac{1}{4}$ | $\frac{1}{4}$ |

   $\frac{1}{4} + \frac{2}{4} =$ _____

2. | $\frac{1}{9}$ | $\frac{1}{9}$ | $\frac{1}{9}$ | $\frac{1}{9}$ | $\frac{1}{9}$ | $\frac{1}{9}$ | $\frac{1}{9}$ | $\frac{1}{9}$ | $\frac{1}{9}$ |

   $\frac{2}{9} + \frac{5}{9} =$ _____

3. | $\frac{1}{6}$ | $\frac{1}{6}$ | $\frac{1}{6}$ | $\frac{1}{6}$ | $\frac{1}{6}$ | $\frac{1}{6}$ |

   $\frac{4}{6} + \frac{1}{6} =$ _____

4. | $\frac{1}{8}$ | $\frac{1}{8}$ | $\frac{1}{8}$ | $\frac{1}{8}$ | $\frac{1}{8}$ | $\frac{1}{8}$ | $\frac{1}{8}$ | $\frac{1}{8}$ |

   $\frac{3}{8} + \frac{5}{8} =$ _____

5. | $\frac{1}{10}$ | $\frac{1}{10}$ | $\frac{1}{10}$ | $\frac{1}{10}$ | $\frac{1}{10}$ | $\frac{1}{10}$ | $\frac{1}{10}$ | $\frac{1}{10}$ | $\frac{1}{10}$ | $\frac{1}{10}$ |

   $\frac{5}{10} + \frac{3}{10} =$ _____

6. | $\frac{1}{12}$ | $\frac{1}{12}$ | $\frac{1}{12}$ | $\frac{1}{12}$ | $\frac{1}{12}$ | $\frac{1}{12}$ | $\frac{1}{12}$ | $\frac{1}{12}$ | $\frac{1}{12}$ | $\frac{1}{12}$ | $\frac{1}{12}$ | $\frac{1}{12}$ |

   $\frac{1}{12} + \frac{5}{12} =$ _____

7. | $\frac{1}{5}$ | $\frac{1}{5}$ | $\frac{1}{5}$ | $\frac{1}{5}$ | $\frac{1}{5}$ |

   $\frac{2}{5} + \frac{1}{5} =$ _____

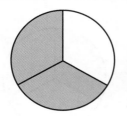

Subtracting Fractions

When the denominators are the same, we only subtract the numerators. The denominator remains the same.

$$\frac{2}{3} - \frac{1}{3} = \frac{1}{3}$$

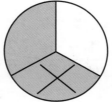

$$\frac{3}{5} - \frac{2}{5} = \frac{1}{5}$$

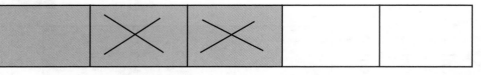

Try These

Shade each drawing and then draw Xs to find the difference.

1. | $\frac{1}{4}$ | $\frac{1}{4}$ | $\frac{1}{4}$ | $\frac{1}{4}$ |

$$\frac{3}{4} - \frac{2}{4} = \rule{2cm}{0.4pt}$$

2. | $\frac{1}{9}$ | $\frac{1}{9}$ | $\frac{1}{9}$ | $\frac{1}{9}$ | $\frac{1}{9}$ | $\frac{1}{9}$ | $\frac{1}{9}$ | $\frac{1}{9}$ | $\frac{1}{9}$ |

$$\frac{5}{9} - \frac{3}{9} = \rule{2cm}{0.4pt}$$

3. | $\frac{1}{6}$ | $\frac{1}{6}$ | $\frac{1}{6}$ | $\frac{1}{6}$ | $\frac{1}{6}$ | $\frac{1}{6}$ |

$$\frac{4}{6} - \frac{2}{6} = \rule{2cm}{0.4pt}$$

4. | $\frac{1}{8}$ | $\frac{1}{8}$ | $\frac{1}{8}$ | $\frac{1}{8}$ | $\frac{1}{8}$ | $\frac{1}{8}$ | $\frac{1}{8}$ | $\frac{1}{8}$ |

$$\frac{7}{8} - \frac{4}{8} = \rule{2cm}{0.4pt}$$

5. | $\frac{1}{10}$ | $\frac{1}{10}$ | $\frac{1}{10}$ | $\frac{1}{10}$ | $\frac{1}{10}$ | $\frac{1}{10}$ | $\frac{1}{10}$ | $\frac{1}{10}$ | $\frac{1}{10}$ | $\frac{1}{10}$ |

$$\frac{8}{10} - \frac{3}{10} = \rule{2cm}{0.4pt}$$

6. | $\frac{1}{12}$ | $\frac{1}{12}$ | $\frac{1}{12}$ | $\frac{1}{12}$ | $\frac{1}{12}$ | $\frac{1}{12}$ | $\frac{1}{12}$ | $\frac{1}{12}$ | $\frac{1}{12}$ | $\frac{1}{12}$ | $\frac{1}{12}$ | $\frac{1}{12}$ |

$$\frac{10}{12} - \frac{3}{12} = \rule{2cm}{0.4pt}$$

7. | $\frac{1}{5}$ | $\frac{1}{5}$ | $\frac{1}{5}$ | $\frac{1}{5}$ | $\frac{1}{5}$ |

$$\frac{4}{5} - \frac{1}{5} = \rule{2cm}{0.4pt}$$

Adding and Subtracting Fractions

Exercise

Find the sum. You may use fraction strips.

1. $\dfrac{1}{4} + \dfrac{2}{4} =$ _____

2. $\dfrac{1}{3} + \dfrac{2}{3} =$ _____

3. $\dfrac{3}{6} + \dfrac{2}{6} =$ _____

4. $\dfrac{1}{10} + \dfrac{4}{10} =$ _____

5. $\dfrac{2}{12} + \dfrac{5}{12} =$ _____

6. $\dfrac{2}{15} + \dfrac{3}{15} =$ _____

7. $\dfrac{1}{5} + \dfrac{1}{5} =$ _____

8. $\dfrac{1}{6} + \dfrac{4}{6} =$ _____

9. $\dfrac{3}{8} + \dfrac{4}{8} =$ _____

10. $\dfrac{2}{7} + \dfrac{2}{7} =$ _____

11. $\dfrac{4}{9} + \dfrac{3}{9} =$ _____

12. $\dfrac{2}{5} + \dfrac{1}{5} =$ _____

Find the difference. You may use fraction strips.

13. $\dfrac{2}{3} - \dfrac{1}{3} =$ _____

14. $\dfrac{3}{4} - \dfrac{1}{4} =$ _____

15. $\dfrac{5}{6} - \dfrac{3}{6} =$ _____

16. $\dfrac{6}{7} - \dfrac{4}{7} =$ _____

17. $\dfrac{6}{8} - \dfrac{1}{8} =$ _____

18. $\dfrac{7}{10} - \dfrac{6}{10} =$ _____

19. $\dfrac{8}{10} - \dfrac{5}{10} =$ _____

20. $\dfrac{7}{8} - \dfrac{4}{8} =$ _____

21. $\dfrac{3}{4} - \dfrac{2}{4} =$ _____

22. $\dfrac{5}{8} - \dfrac{3}{8} =$ _____

23. $\dfrac{7}{12} - \dfrac{3}{12} =$ _____

24. $\dfrac{4}{5} - \dfrac{2}{5} =$ _____

Solve.

1. The farmer plowed $\frac{1}{5}$ of a field one afternoon.

   The next day he plowed $\frac{2}{5}$ of the field.

   What fraction of the field has he plowed altogether?   _____

2. In the problem above,
   what fraction of the field
   remains to be plowed?   _____

3. If a week is 7 days, what fraction of a week is 2 days?   _____

4. If $\frac{5}{7}$ of a week is devoted to work,

   what fraction of the week is left?   _____

5. Mark ran $\frac{7}{8}$ of a mile. Richard ran $\frac{3}{8}$ of a mile.

   How much farther did Mark run than Richard?   _____

6. Marie ate $\frac{1}{6}$ of the pizza. Margaret ate $\frac{2}{6}$ of the pizza.

   How much of the pizza did the two girls eat?   _____

7. How much of the pizza was left after the girls finished?   _____

8. The saint spent $\frac{2}{12}$ of her time in prayer and

   $\frac{4}{12}$ of her time in good works. How much of her

   time did she spend on prayer and good works?   _____

If you have not already done so, complete the Skills Tests for Objective #8 on p. 202. When you have
successfully completed the tests, you may check them off on your objectives list on page 186.

Review

Write the equivalent fraction for each. You may use the fraction strips.

1. $\dfrac{2}{6} = \dfrac{?}{12}$ _____

2. $\dfrac{4}{5} = \dfrac{?}{10}$ _____

Multiply each fraction by a form of one to determine an equivalent fraction.

3. $\dfrac{2}{3} \times$ ___ = _____

4. $\dfrac{3}{5} \times$ ___ = _____

5. $\dfrac{1}{6} \times$ ___ = _____

Compare:

6. $\dfrac{4}{5}$ ◯ $\dfrac{3}{5}$

7. $\dfrac{2}{4}$ ◯ $\dfrac{3}{4}$

8. $\dfrac{1}{3}$ ◯ $\dfrac{3}{3}$

9.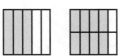

$\dfrac{2}{4}$ ◯ $\dfrac{1}{2}$

10.

$\dfrac{3}{5}$ ◯ $\dfrac{8}{10}$

11.

$\dfrac{1}{2}$ ◯ $\dfrac{3}{8}$

Find part of a number.

12. $\dfrac{1}{3}$ of 18 _____

13. $\dfrac{1}{4}$ of 28 _____

14. $\dfrac{1}{5}$ of 30 _____

15. $\dfrac{2}{4}$ of 16 = _____

16. $\dfrac{2}{3}$ of 15 = _____

17. $\dfrac{3}{4}$ of 12 = _____

18. $\dfrac{4}{5}$ of 25 = _____

Write the mixed number for each.

19. 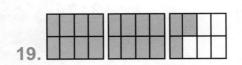 _____

20. _____

133

Find each sum or difference. Watch the signs.

1. $\begin{array}{r}16\\-\ 9\\\hline\end{array}$
2. $\begin{array}{r}3\\+2\\\hline\end{array}$
3. $\begin{array}{r}6\\-2\\\hline\end{array}$
4. $\begin{array}{r}1\\+6\\\hline\end{array}$
5. $\begin{array}{r}8\\-1\\\hline\end{array}$
6. $\begin{array}{r}1\\+1\\\hline\end{array}$

7. $\begin{array}{r}7\\+4\\\hline\end{array}$
8. $\begin{array}{r}4\\-1\\\hline\end{array}$
9. $\begin{array}{r}6\\+2\\\hline\end{array}$
10. $\begin{array}{r}11\\-\ 4\\\hline\end{array}$
11. $\begin{array}{r}7\\+9\\\hline\end{array}$
12. $\begin{array}{r}8\\-6\\\hline\end{array}$

Multiply.

13. $\begin{array}{r}7\\\times6\\\hline\end{array}$
14. $\begin{array}{r}6\\\times2\\\hline\end{array}$
15. $\begin{array}{r}5\\\times9\\\hline\end{array}$
16. $\begin{array}{r}5\\\times0\\\hline\end{array}$
17. $\begin{array}{r}2\\\times4\\\hline\end{array}$
18. $\begin{array}{r}9\\\times1\\\hline\end{array}$

19. $\begin{array}{r}8\\\times2\\\hline\end{array}$
20. $\begin{array}{r}8\\\times8\\\hline\end{array}$
21. $\begin{array}{r}8\\\times5\\\hline\end{array}$
22. $\begin{array}{r}7\\\times4\\\hline\end{array}$
23. $\begin{array}{r}5\\\times8\\\hline\end{array}$
24. $\begin{array}{r}2\\\times7\\\hline\end{array}$

25. $\begin{array}{r}460\\\times\ \ \ 4\\\hline\end{array}$
26. $\begin{array}{r}329\\\times\ \ \ 5\\\hline\end{array}$
27. $\begin{array}{r}198\\\times\ \ \ 6\\\hline\end{array}$
28. $\begin{array}{r}748\\\times\ \ \ 9\\\hline\end{array}$

Add.

29. $\begin{array}{r}128\\376\\532\\+\ 111\\\hline\end{array}$
30. $\begin{array}{r}586\\428\\821\\+\ 764\\\hline\end{array}$
31. $\begin{array}{r}2875\\6781\\5896\\+6434\\\hline\end{array}$
32. $\begin{array}{r}8654\\1298\\1385\\+1830\\\hline\end{array}$

33. $\begin{array}{r}324\\+\ 472\\\hline\end{array}$
34. $\begin{array}{r}589\\+\ 723\\\hline\end{array}$
35. $\begin{array}{r}1242\\+1596\\\hline\end{array}$
36. $\begin{array}{r}3428\\+3178\\\hline\end{array}$

Fractions and Decimals

Like fractions, we can use **decimals**
to show parts of a whole

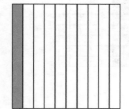

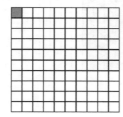

$\frac{1}{10}$ = 0.1
one tenth

$\frac{1}{100}$ = 0.01
one hundredth

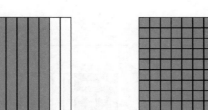

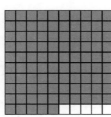

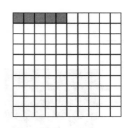

$\frac{8}{10}$ = 0.8
eight tenths

$\frac{95}{100}$ = 0.95
ninety-five
hundredths

$\frac{2}{10}$ = 0.2
two tenths

$\frac{5}{100}$ = 0.05
five hundredths

Try These

Write the fraction, the decimal, and the word name for each.

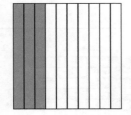

1.

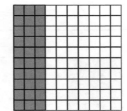

2.

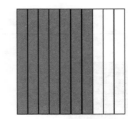

3.

fraction _____

decimal _____

_____

fraction _____

decimal _____

_____

fraction _____

decimal _____

_____

135

4.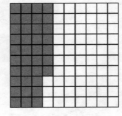

fraction _____

decimal _____

_____

5.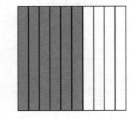

fraction _____

decimal _____

_____

6.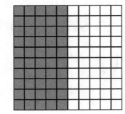

fraction _____

decimal _____

_____

7.

fraction _____

decimal _____

_____

8.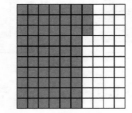

fraction _____

decimal _____

_____

9.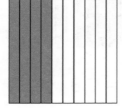

fraction _____

decimal _____

_____

10.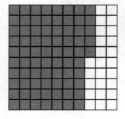

fraction _____

decimal _____

_____

11.

fraction _____

decimal _____

_____

12.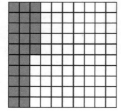

fraction _____

decimal _____

_____

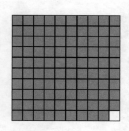

Writing Decimals

$$\underline{\quad 0 \quad} . \underline{\quad 9 \quad} \underline{\quad 9 \quad}$$
$$\text{ones} \qquad \text{tenths} \quad \text{hundredths}$$

When writing decimals, we write a zero before the decimal point to show that there are no ones. Then we write the tenths and hundredths,

Exercise

Write the decimal for each fraction. Be sure to write the 0 in the ones place.

1. $\dfrac{3}{10}$ _____

2. $\dfrac{7}{10}$ _____

3. $\dfrac{5}{10}$ _____

4. $\dfrac{1}{100}$ _____

5. $\dfrac{23}{100}$ _____

6. $\dfrac{59}{100}$ _____

7. $\dfrac{2}{10}$ _____

8. $\dfrac{8}{10}$ _____

9. $\dfrac{6}{10}$ _____

10. $\dfrac{4}{100}$ _____

11. $\dfrac{55}{100}$ _____

12. $\dfrac{99}{100}$ _____

Write the decimal for the word name. Write the 0 in the ones place.

13. one tenth

14. five tenths

15. nine tenths

_____

_____

_____

16. seven hundredths

17. twenty hundredths

18. fourteen hundredths

_____

_____

_____

137

Exercise

Write each decimal as a fraction.

1. 0.3 _____

2. 0.5 _____

3. 0.7 _____

4. 0.21 _____

5. 0.35 _____

6. 0.75 _____

7. 0.4 _____

8. 0.6 _____

9. 0.8 _____

10. 0.99 _____

11. 0.01 _____

12. 0.11 _____

Write the fraction for the word name.

13. three tenths

_____

14. five tenths

_____

15. seven tenths

_____

16. seven hundredths

_____

17. twenty hundredths

_____

18. fourteen hundredths

_____

Objective #9 – Decimals and Fractions

The student will be able to write tenths and hundredths in both decimal and fraction form and be able to add and subtract tenths and hundredths in decimal form and will demonstrate his mastery by completing the Skill Test for Objective #9 on p. 203 quickly and accurately.

Fractions and Decimals

Mixed Decimals

$$5 \quad 3 \quad . \quad 2 \quad 7$$

tens   ones   . tenths   hundredths

The **place** of a **digit** determines its **value**.

5 tens 3 ones . 2 tenths 7 hundredths = 53.27

Write the decimal and word name for $21\frac{55}{100}$

2 tens 1 one . 5 tenths 5 hundredths = 21.55

twenty-one and fifty-five hundredths

Exercise

Write each mixed number as a mixed decimal.

1. $3\frac{4}{10}$ _____

2. $5\frac{8}{10}$ _____

3. $7\frac{1}{10}$ _____

4. $21\frac{34}{100}$ _____

5. $35\frac{36}{100}$ _____

6. $75\frac{28}{100}$ _____

7. $4\frac{9}{10}$ _____

8. $6\frac{7}{10}$ _____

9. $8\frac{2}{10}$ _____

10. $99\frac{92}{100}$ _____

11. $11\frac{20}{100}$ _____

12. $15\frac{90}{100}$ _____

13. $55\frac{5}{100}$ _____

14. $9\frac{7}{10}$ _____

15. $22\frac{8}{100}$ _____

16. $80\frac{1}{100}$ _____

17. $17\frac{75}{100}$ _____

18. $15\frac{3}{10}$ _____

Mixed Decimals

The **place** of a **digit** determines its **value.**

Write the word name for 7.99

Write the whole number part in words.

seven

For the decimal point we write "and".

seven and

Look at the number after the decimal point. Decide whether it is tenths or hundredths, and write that number.

seven and ninety-nine hundredths

Write the word name for 12.7   twelve and seven tenths

Exercise

Write the word name for each mixed decimal.

1. 3.7

    _____

2. 21.9

    _____

3. 4.23

    _____

4. 9.8

    _____

5. 50.5

    _____

6. 7.44

    _____

7. 75.0

    _____

Comparing Decimals

The first thing to check when comparing decimal numbers is the number of digits to the left of the decimal place. The number with the most digits is the larger number.

Example: Compare 24.56 and 2.99

We see that 24.56 has 2 digits to the left of the decimal point and 2.99 has only 1 digit to the left of the decimal point.   24.56 is greater than 2.99

If both numbers have the same number of digits to the left of the decimal point, then we compare the digits with the greatest place value. We start on the left and compare.

Example: Compare 3.56 and 2.99

We see that each number has one digit to the left of the decimal.

3.56 has 3 in the ones place, and 2.99 has 2 in the ones place.

Three is more than two so: 3.56 is greater than 2.99

Exercise

Compare each set of numbers and circle the one that is greater.

1.   4.79   and   3.52   2.   32.29   and   69.17

3.   9.98   and   7.78   4.   26.16   and   32.54

5.   1.23   and   0.78   6.   9.87   and   8.07

7.   0.97   and   3.1   8.   0.06   and   6.0

9.   3.59   and   0.13   10.   4.3   and   7.8

11.   29.6   and   96.2   12.   4.29   and   32.15

Comparing Decimals

If the numbers are equal on the left side of the decimal point then we look to the right side of the decimal point beginning with the tenths place.

Example: Compare 0.56 and 0.73

ones.	tenths	hundredths
0.	5	6

We see that the numbers are equal on the left side of the decimal point.

ones.	tenths	hundredths
0.	7	3

We begin by comparing the tenths place.

Seven tenths is more than five tenths   0.73 is greater than 0.56

Example: Compare 0.76 and 0.73

ones.	tenths	hundredths
0.	7	6

We see that the numbers are equal on the left side of the decimal point.

ones.	tenths	hundredths
0.	7	3

We begin by comparing the tenths place.

Seven tenths and seven tenths are the same so we move to the hundredths. Six hundredths is more than three hundredths.

0.76 is greater than 0.73

Exercise

Compare each set of numbers and circle the one that is greater.

1.   0.79   and   3.52   2.   0.29   and   0.17

3.   0.98   and   0.78   4.   1.16   and   1.54

5.   0.23   and   0.78   6.   0.87   and   0.07

7.   0.97   and   3.1   8.   3.06   and   3.60

9.   0.59   and   0.13   10.   4.35   and   4.8

11.   0.6   and   0.08   12.   0.29   and   0.15

Comparing Decimals with a Number Line

You can use a number line to compare decimals.

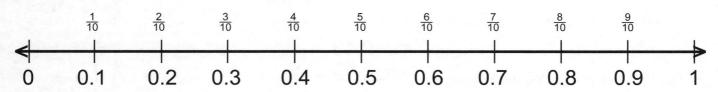

Numbers to the right are greater than numbers to the left.

is less than <	**Remember**	is greater than >

(Tip: The small end should point to the smaller number.)

Exercise

Compare. Write < or > in the circle. You may use the number line.

1. 0.3 ◯ 0.1   2. 0.2 ◯ 0.1

3. 0.7 ◯ 0.9   4. 0.6 ◯ $\frac{2}{10}$

5. 0.5 ◯ $\frac{3}{10}$ 6. 4.1 ◯ 4.5

7. 0.3 ◯ 0.4   8. $\frac{4}{10}$ ◯ 0.8

9. 0.1 ◯ 0.9   10. 3.1 ◯ 3.3

11. 0.1 ◯ $\frac{5}{10}$ 12. 8.4 ◯ 2.2

13. 6.5 ◯ 9.3   14. $\frac{9}{10}$ ◯ 0.1

15. 3.9 ◯ 3.2   16. 7.8 ◯ 7.0

17. $\frac{7}{10}$ ◯ 0.8   18. 0.1 ◯ $\frac{2}{10}$

19. 2.3 ◯ 2.6   20. 1.5 ◯ 1.3

Adding Decimals

The first thing to do when adding decimals is to line up the decimal points.

Add: 2.43 + 5.59

First we rewrite vertically:

$$\begin{array}{r} 2.43 \\ +\ 5.59 \\ \hline \end{array}$$

Make sure to line up the decimal points.

$$\begin{array}{r} {\scriptstyle 1\ 1} \\ 2.43 \\ +\ 5.59 \\ \hline 8.02 \end{array}$$

Then we add as usual and put the decimal point in the sum.

Exercise

Add.

1. $\begin{array}{r} 1.6 \\ +\ 2.2 \\ \hline \end{array}$
2. $\begin{array}{r} 2.5 \\ +\ 3.7 \\ \hline \end{array}$
3. $\begin{array}{r} 7.2 \\ +\ 1.4 \\ \hline \end{array}$
4. $\begin{array}{r} 7.4 \\ +\ 3.7 \\ \hline \end{array}$

5. $\begin{array}{r} 0.12 \\ +\ 0.35 \\ \hline \end{array}$
6. $\begin{array}{r} 0.87 \\ +\ 0.92 \\ \hline \end{array}$
7. $\begin{array}{r} 0.50 \\ +\ 0.59 \\ \hline \end{array}$
8. $\begin{array}{r} 4.5 \\ +\ 5.5 \\ \hline \end{array}$

9. $\begin{array}{r} 2.47 \\ +\ 1.34 \\ \hline \end{array}$
10. $\begin{array}{r} 2.43 \\ +\ 5.59 \\ \hline \end{array}$
11. $\begin{array}{r} 4.03 \\ +\ 1.92 \\ \hline \end{array}$
12. $\begin{array}{r} 41.13 \\ +\ 23.38 \\ \hline \end{array}$

13. $\begin{array}{r} 31.14 \\ +\ 21.83 \\ \hline \end{array}$
14. $\begin{array}{r} 34.76 \\ +\ 51.63 \\ \hline \end{array}$
15. $\begin{array}{r} 0.60 \\ +\ 0.59 \\ \hline \end{array}$
16. $\begin{array}{r} 0.6 \\ +\ 1.7 \\ \hline \end{array}$

17. $\begin{array}{r} 0.2 \\ +\ 0.5 \\ \hline \end{array}$
18. $\begin{array}{r} 0.3 \\ +\ 0.7 \\ \hline \end{array}$
19. $\begin{array}{r} 30.41 \\ +\ 25.69 \\ \hline \end{array}$
20. $\begin{array}{r} 14.03 \\ +\ 21.92 \\ \hline \end{array}$

Subtracting Decimals

The first thing to do when subtracting decimals is to line up the decimal points.

Subtract: 7.42 – 3.21

First we rewrite vertically:

$$\begin{array}{r} 7.42 \\ -\ 3.21 \\ \hline \end{array}$$

Make sure to line up the decimal points.

Then we subtract as usual and put the decimal point in the difference.

$$\begin{array}{r} 7.42 \\ -\ 3.21 \\ \hline 4.21 \end{array}$$

Exercise

Subtract.

1.
$$\begin{array}{r} 8.50 \\ -\ 3.41 \\ \hline \end{array}$$

2.
$$\begin{array}{r} 9.32 \\ -\ 1.88 \\ \hline \end{array}$$

3.
$$\begin{array}{r} 8.84 \\ -\ 2.63 \\ \hline \end{array}$$

4.
$$\begin{array}{r} 7.62 \\ -\ 5.39 \\ \hline \end{array}$$

5.
$$\begin{array}{r} 0.8 \\ -\ 0.5 \\ \hline \end{array}$$

6.
$$\begin{array}{r} 6.00 \\ -\ 2.99 \\ \hline \end{array}$$

7.
$$\begin{array}{r} 1.4 \\ -\ 0.7 \\ \hline \end{array}$$

8.
$$\begin{array}{r} 8.0 \\ -\ 5.3 \\ \hline \end{array}$$

9.
$$\begin{array}{r} 4.55 \\ -\ 3.05 \\ \hline \end{array}$$

10.
$$\begin{array}{r} 9.43 \\ -\ 7.76 \\ \hline \end{array}$$

11.
$$\begin{array}{r} 6.87 \\ -\ 4.29 \\ \hline \end{array}$$

12.
$$\begin{array}{r} 7.00 \\ -\ 2.69 \\ \hline \end{array}$$

13.
$$\begin{array}{r} 5.5 \\ -\ 3.7 \\ \hline \end{array}$$

14.
$$\begin{array}{r} 5.9 \\ -\ 4.2 \\ \hline \end{array}$$

15.
$$\begin{array}{r} 6.2 \\ -\ 5.8 \\ \hline \end{array}$$

16.
$$\begin{array}{r} 8.3 \\ -\ 2.7 \\ \hline \end{array}$$

Adding and Subtracting Decimals

Exercise

Add.

1. 6.4
    + 2.2

2. 2.3
    + 4.3

3. 8.0
    + 6.7

4. 5.3
    + 4.7

5. 0.12
    + 0.24

6. 0.35
    + 0.27

7. 1.6
    + 3.8

8. 7.5
    + 3.6

9. 3.64
    + 2.21

10. 4.55
    + 2.75

11. 4.28
    + 3.72

12. 7.19
    + 2.81

Subtract.

13. 8.27
    − 3.19

14. 8.7
    − 5.6

15. 6.20
    − 2.07

16. 4.06
    − 0.42

17. 6.9
    − 2.5

18. 8.02
    − 5.46

19. 6.7
    − 3.4

20. 7.4
    − 2.3

21. 6.30
    − 2.52

22. 9.3
    − 2.9

23. 6.24
    − 5.88

24. 9.20
    − 5.84

Adding and Subtracting Decimals

146

Exercise

Solve.

1. It is 3.7 miles to Grandmother's house and 2.1 miles to Uncle John's. How much further is it to Grandmother's than it is to Uncle John's? _____

2. John and Peter walk to Mass everyday. They walk 1.05 miles down Baker Street to the church, and 1.20 miles back home on Cathedral Avenue. How many miles altogether do they walk? _____

3. John and Anthony were collecting newspapers for recycling. John collected 10.6 pounds and Anthony collected 11.2 pounds. How many pounds did they collect altogether? _____

4. Maria got 7 out of 10 of her religion questions right. How would this be written as a decimal? _____

5. What decimal would tell the portion of questions she answered incorrectly? _____

6. Maria must read 5 chapters before the final exam on the Commandments, and each one is 10 pages. What decimal representation of the chapters has she read if she finished 3 full chapters and 4 pages of the next one? _____

7. What mixed decimal would represent the chapter amount she has left to read? _____

8. During the Pro-Life March, Joe walked 2.6 kilometers and Peter walked 2.9 kilometers. Who walked further? _____

9. How much further did he walk? _____

10. Mark was trying to raise $100 towards his trip to Fatima with Fr. Fox. So far he had $35. What decimal part of his goal had he reached? _____

11. A statue of St. Joseph costs $7.82 and a statue of St. Elizabeth Seton costs $5.79. How much more does the St. Joseph statue cost? _____

Problem Solving with Decimals

If you have not already done so, complete the Skills Tests for Objective #9 on pp. 203. When you have successfully completed the tests you may check them off on your objectives list on page 186.

Write the decimal for each fraction. Be sure to write the 0 in the ones place.

1. $\frac{5}{10}$ _____

2. $\frac{4}{10}$ _____

3. $\frac{1}{10}$ _____

4. $\frac{49}{100}$ _____

5. $\frac{4}{100}$ _____

6. $\frac{10}{100}$ _____

Write the decimal for the word name. Write the 0 in the ones place.

7. three tenths

8. five hundredths

9. thirty hundredths

_____   _____   _____

Write each decimal as a fraction.

10. 0.1 _____

11. 0.6 _____

12. 0.9 _____

13. 0.25 _____

14. 0.89 _____

15. 0.01 _____

Write each mixed number as a mixed decimal.

16. $2\frac{7}{10}$ _____

17. $3\frac{9}{10}$ _____

18. $9\frac{1}{10}$ _____

19. $33\frac{7}{100}$ _____

20. $14\frac{50}{100}$ _____

21. $97\frac{35}{100}$ _____

Compare. Write < or > in the circle. You may use the number line.

22. 0.4 $\bigcirc$ 0.1

23. 0.2 $\bigcirc$ 0.7

24. 0.7 $\bigcirc$ 0.9

25. 0.4 $\bigcirc$ $\frac{2}{10}$

Decimal Review

Plane Figures

A **plane figure** is a figure that can be contained in a **plane**.

A **plane** is a flat surface extending in all directions without limit.

For example, we can think of a flat surface, like a sheet of paper or a table top. They would be part of a **plane**. A **plane** only has **two dimensions**. That is why we call it flat. A **plane** has **length** and **width** but no **depth**. Our world has **three dimensions**: **length**, **width**, and **depth**. We call it **space**.

Here are some plane figures. Can you name them?

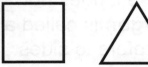 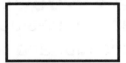

Here are some drawings of some solids. Can you name them.

What is the difference between a plane figure and a solid?
A plane figure is in two dimensions. A solid is in three dimensions.

We say an enclosed plane figure has **area** and a solid has **volume**.

Study the figures and the names below.

 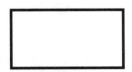

square   triangle   rectangle   circle   pentagon   hexagon

   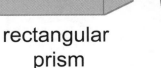 

cube   pyramid   rectangular prism   sphere   cylinder   cone

Polygons and Circles

A **polygon** is a **closed plane figure** with straight **line segments** for sides.
By closed we mean with no openings.

closed	closed	closed
open	open	open

A circle is a closed figure but it is not a **polygon** because it does not have straight line segments for sides. A four-sided **polygon** is called a **quadrilateral**. The prefix *quad* means four and *lateral* refers to sides.

Try These

Is each figure a polygon? Write *Yes* or *No*.

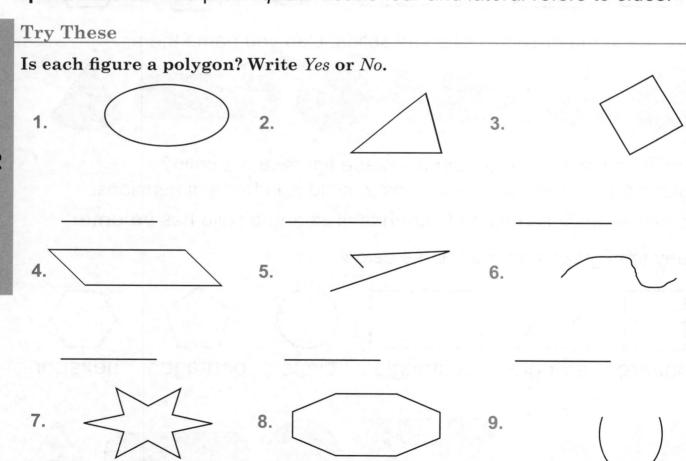

1.

2.

3.

4.

5.

6.

7.

8.

9.

Polygons

150

Points, Lines, Rays, and Line Segments

A **point** is a location in space.
We represent it like this: •

A **line** is straight. It is a set of points that go on **infinitely** (forever) in both directions. It has no **endpoints**.
We represent it like this: ⟷

A **ray** is a part of a line that goes on **infinitely** (forever) in one direction. It has one **endpoint**.
We represent it like this: •———→

A **line segment** is a part of a line with two **endpoints**. We represent it like this: •———•

Try These

Write the name for each: line, line segment, ray, or none of these.

1.

2.

3.

_____   _____   _____

4.

5.

6.

_____   _____   _____

7.

8.

9.

_____   _____   _____

More Lines: Horizontal, Vertical, Parallel, and Intersecting

A **horizontal** line goes straight across.

A **vertical** line goes straight up and down.

Lines that **intersect** are lines that meet at one point.

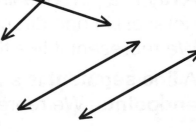

Parallel lines are lines in the same plane that do not meet.

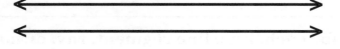

Try These

Write whether each pair of lines are parallel or intersect.

1.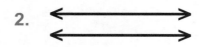

2.

3.

_____   _____   _____

4.

5.

6.

_____   _____   _____

7. Draw a set of parallel lines.

8. Draw a set of intersecting lines.

More Lines

152

Angles

An **angle** is formed by two rays or line segments with the same endpoint.

A **right angle** forms a square corner. This is the symbol for a right angle: ⌐

An **acute angle** is less than a right angle.

An **obtuse angle** is greater than a right angle.

If two lines, rays, or line segments form a right angle then the lines are **perpendicular**.

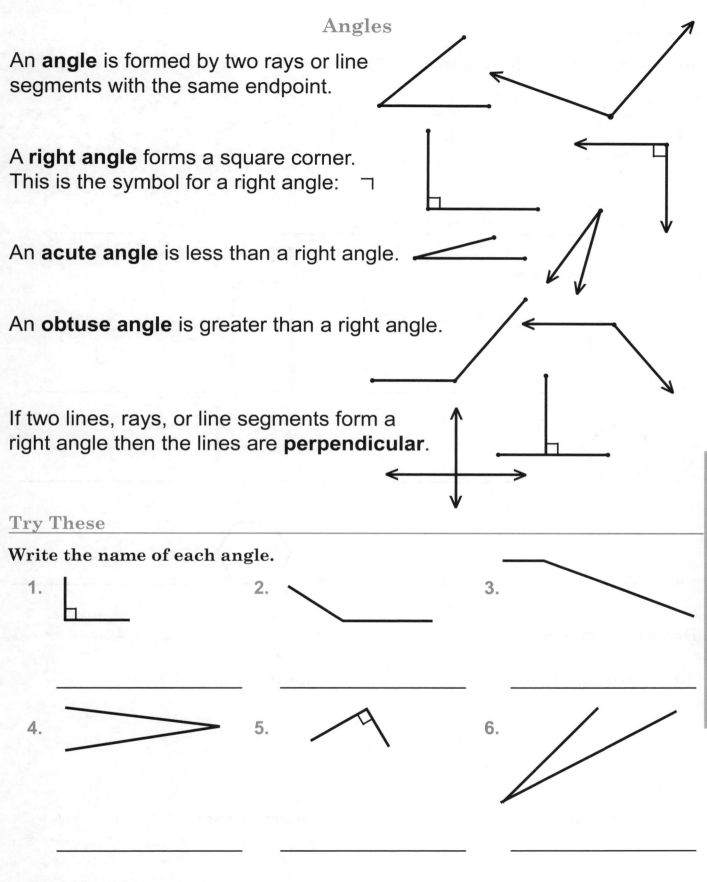

Try These

Write the name of each angle.

1. _____

2. _____

3. _____

4. _____

5. _____

6. _____

7. Draw an acute angle.

8. Draw an obtuse angle.

Angles

153

Exercise

How many right angles are in each figure?

1. 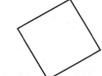 _____

2. _____

3. _____

Write the name of each figure.

4. _____

5. _____

6. _____

7. _____

8. _____

9. _____

Draw the items indicated.

10. a horizontal line

11. parallel lines

12. a right angle

13. an acute angle

14. an obtuse angle

15. a line segment

16. a vertical line

17. intersecting lines

18. a ray

How many angles does each figure have?

19.

20.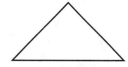

21.

_____

_____

_____

22.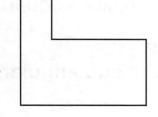

23.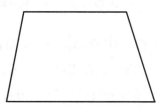

24.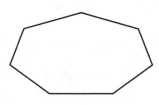

_____

_____

_____

Divide.

25. 8)645

26. 9)279

27. 2)164

28. 5)292

A **triangle** is 3-sided polygon. Triangles are widely used in everyday life. Look around and see how many triangles you can identify. Triangles are often used for decoration and ornamentation. They can also be used to measure heights and distances. Triangles are also used as an important part of construction. A triangle is a very strong and stable shape.

There are several different kinds of triangles. We can name triangles by the length of their sides. We can also name triangles by the size of their angles.

If all the sides of a triangle are the same length, we call it **equilateral**.
If two sides of a triangle are the same length, we call it **isosceles**.
If none of the sides of a triangle are the same length, we call it **scalene**.

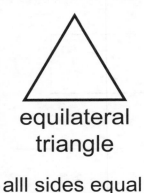
equilateral
triangle

alll sides equal

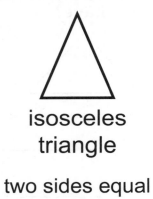
isosceles
triangle

two sides equal

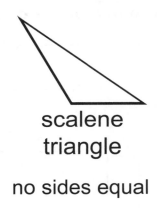
scalene
triangle

no sides equal

We can also name triangles by the size of their angles.
If all the angles of a triangle are the same size, we call it **equiangular**.
An **equiangular** triangle is also **equilateral**.

If a triangle has one right angle, it is called a **right triangle**.
If all three angles of a triangle are acute, we call it an **acute triangle**.
If one angle of a triangle is obtuse, we call it an **obtuse triangle**.

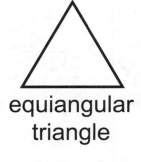
equiangular
triangle

all angles equal

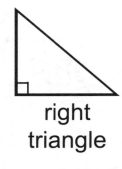
right
triangle

one right angle

acute
triangle

all acute angles

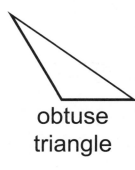
obtuse
triangle

one obtuse angle

Try These

Write the name of each triangle according to its sides.

1.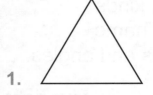

_____

2.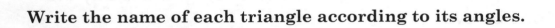

_____

3.

_____

4.

_____

Write the name of each triangle according to its angles.

5.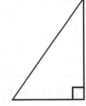

_____

6.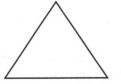

_____

7.

_____

Use two words to describe each triangle by its sides and angles.

8.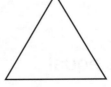

_____

_____

9.

_____

_____

10.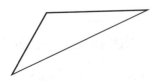

_____

_____

Triangles

157

Quadrilaterals

A **quadrilateral** is a 4-sided polygon.

There are several different kinds of **quadrilaterals**. We can name quadrilaterals by their sides and angles.

If all the sides are equal and it has four right angles, it is a **square**. If the opposite sides are equal, and it has four right angles, then it is a **rectangle**. That means that all squares are rectangles but not all rectangles are squares. If the opposite sides are equal to one another and parallel then we have a **parallelogram**. If all the sides are equal to one another and the opposite sides are parallel then we have a **rhombus**. If there is only one pair of parallel sides then it is a **trapezoid**. A rhombus is always a parallelogram but not every parallelogram is a rhombus. A square is a parallelogram and a rhombus. A rectangle is a parallelogram. Study the figures and definitions below.

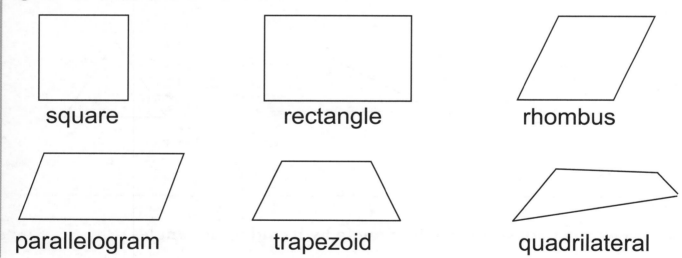

square   rectangle   rhombus

parallelogram   trapezoid   quadrilateral

quadrilateral - a polygon with four sides

square - a quadrilateral with four right angles and all side equal

rectangle - a quadrilateral with four right angles and opposite side equal

rhombus - a quadrilateral with all sides equal and opposite sides parallel

parallelogram - a quadrilateral with opposite sides equal and opposite sides parallel

trapezoid - quadrilateral with only one pair of parallel sides

Try These

Write the name of each quadrilateral.

1.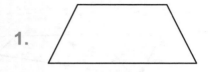

_____

2.

_____

3.

4.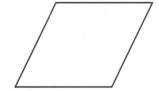

5.

_____   _____   _____

Write _Yes_ **or** _No_.

6. Is every square a rectangle? Tell why or why not.   _____

7. Is every rectangle a square? Tell why or why not.   _____

8. Is every parallelogram a rectangle? Tell why or why not.   _____

9. Is every rectangle a parallelogram? Tell why or why not.   _____

10. Is a square a parallelogram? Tell why or why not.   _____

Draw:

11. **a trapezoid**   12. **a rhombus**   13. **a quadrilateral**

Congruent Figures

Congruent figures have the same size and shape. Congruent means "the same." Look at the figures below.

congruent   congruent   not congruent

Try These

Circle the congruent figures in each row.

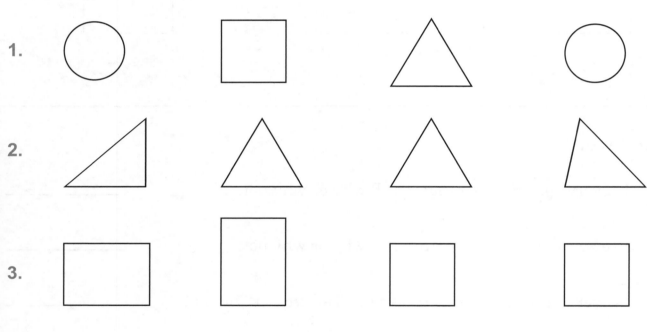

1.

2.

3.

4.

5.

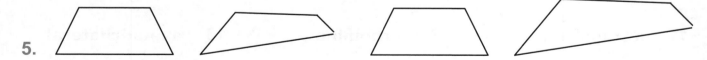

6.

Congruent Figures

Similar Figures

Similar figures have the same shape. They may or may not be the same size. This means that if two figures are congruent then they are similar, but if they are similar, they may or may not be congruent.

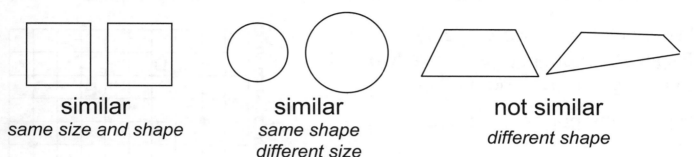

similar	similar	not similar
same size and shape	*same shape* *different size*	*different shape*

Try These

Circle the similar figures in each row.

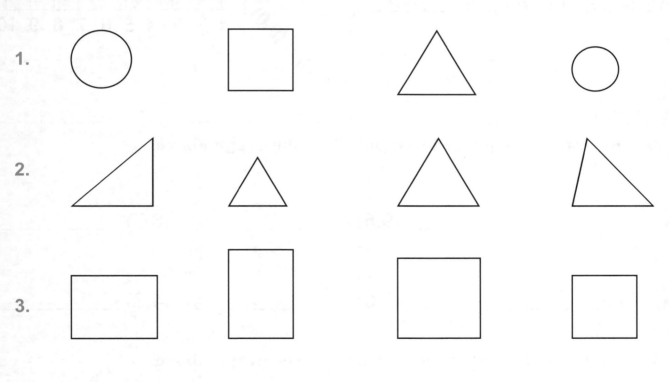

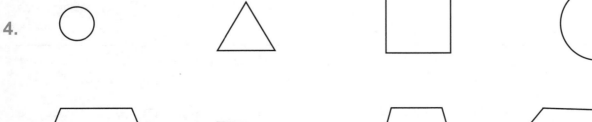

Ordered Pairs

Ordered pairs are pairs of numbers that show the location of points on a **coordinate grid**. The first number of an ordered pair is the **horizontal** distance from the **origin**, and the second number is the **vertical** distance from the **origin**. The **origin** is indicated by the **coordinates (0,0)**.

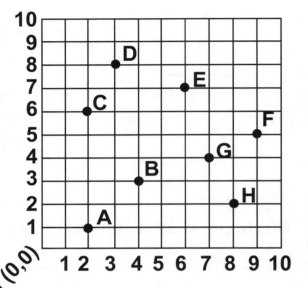

What point is at location (2,1)?
Begin at the origin **(0,0)**. move two units to the right. Move one unit up.

What is the point? ____**A**____

What is the location of point H?
What is the horizontal coordinate for H? 8
What is the vertical coordinate for H? 2

What is the ordered pair? ____**(8,2)**____

Try These

Write the letter for each ordered pair. Use the graph above.

1. (7,4) _____
2. (9,5) _____
3. (6,7) _____

4. (3,8) _____
5. (2,6) _____
6. (4,3) _____

Write the ordered pair for each letter. Use the graph above.

7. B _____
8. C _____
9. D _____

10. E _____
11. F _____
12. G _____

Exercise

Write the letter for each ordered pair.
Use the graph to the right.

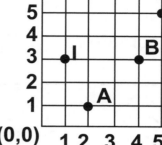

1. (7,4) _____
2. (9,5) _____

3. (6,7) _____
4. (3,8) _____

5. (2,6) _____
6. (4,3) _____

7. (1,9) _____
8. (8,2) _____
9. (2,1) _____

10. (1,3) _____
11. (5,5) _____
12. (9,9) _____

Write the ordered pair for each letter. Use the graph below.

13. A _____
14. B _____
15. C _____

16. D _____
17. E _____
18. F _____

19. G _____
20. H _____
21. I _____

22. J _____
23. K _____

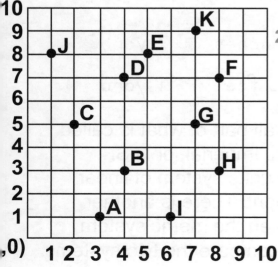

Ordered Pairs

163

Linear Measure

This is 1 inch. in. means **inch**.

This is 1 centimeter. **cm** means **centimeter**.

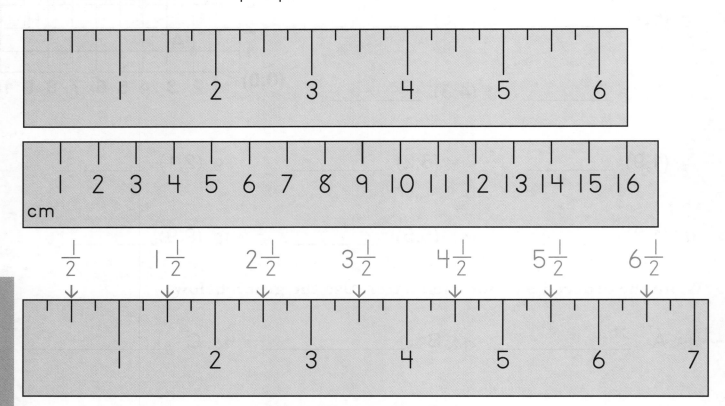

Some Facts to Know

A **foot** is 12 inches.
A ruler is usually a **foot** long.

12 inches = 1 foot

A **mile** is 5280 feet.
A **mile** is 1760 yards.

5280 feet = 1 mile
1760 yards = 1 mile

A **yard** is 36 inches.
There are 3 feet in a **yard**.
A yardstick is a **yard** long.

36 inches = 1 yard
3 feet = 1 yard

These are all part of what is called the English, Imperial, or U.S. customary units system of linear measurement. There is another system called the metric system (SI). Let's compare the two systems.

Measurement

A centimeter is approximately $\frac{4}{10}$ (0.4) of an inch.
There are about 2½ cm in an inch.

A meter is about 39 inches.
A meter is a little more than a yard.
(approximately $1\frac{9}{100}$ (1.09) of a yard)

A kilometer is approximately $\frac{62}{100}$ (0.62) of a mile.

There are **100 centimeters** (cm) in **1 meter** (m).
There are **1000 millimeters** (mm) in **1 meter**.
There are **10 millimeters** in **1 centimeter**.
There are **1000 meters** in **1 kilometer** (km).

10mm = 1 cm	There are about $2\frac{1}{2}$ cm in an inch.
100cm = 1 m	A meter is about 39 inches.
1000mm = 1 m	A meter is a little more than a yard.
1000m = 1 km	There are about $1\frac{6}{10}$ km in a mile.

Try These

1. How many inches are in a foot? _____

2. How many feet are in a yard? _____

3. About how many centimeters are in an inch? _____

4. About how many inches are in a meter? _____

5. How many feet are in a mile? _____

6. How many inches are in a yard? _____

Measure each of the following with an inch ruler.

1. _____ in.

2. _____ in.

3. _____ in.

4. _____ in.

5. _____ in.

6. _____ in.

Measure each of the following with a centimeter ruler.

7. _____ cm

8. _____ cm

9. _____ cm

10. _____ cm

11. _____ cm

12. _____ cm

Measurement

Perimeter

Perimeter is the distance around a figure. To find the perimeter we add the lengths of the sides. The distance around a circle is called its circumference. In a square, all the sides are the same length.

What is the perimeter of the figure?

We add up all the sides:

4m + 4m + 4m + 4m = 16m

The perimeter is 16m.

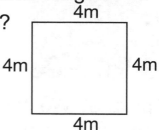

Try These

Find the perimeter of each of the figures. (Add all the sides)

1.
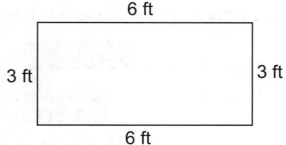

_____

2.
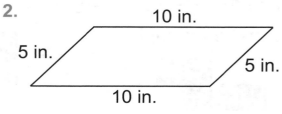

_____

3.
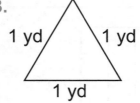

_____

4.
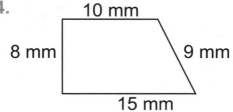

_____

5.
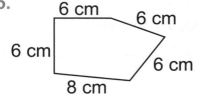

_____

6.
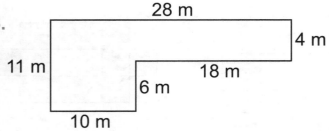

_____

7.
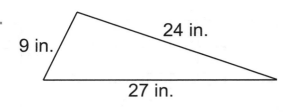

_____

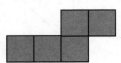

Area

Area is the number of square units needed to cover the surface of a plane figure. To find the area we calculate or count the number of units. Look at the picture to the left. Count the number of square units to find the area.

What is the area of the picture? We can count the number of units or since the figure is rectangular, we can use a formula. The formula for finding the area of a rectangular figure is length times width.

The picture is 9 units long and 6 units wide. Because we know our multiplication table we know that 9 × 6 = 54. If we count the units we will also find that there are 54. The area of the picture is 54 square units.

Study these examples:

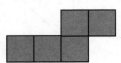

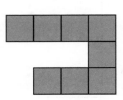

The area is 5 square units.	The area is 5 square units.	The area is 8 square units.

Area

Exercise

Find the area of each of the figures.

1.

_____ square units

2.
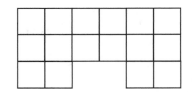

_____ square units

3.
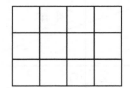

4.
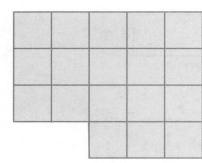

5.
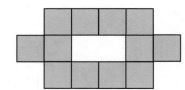

_____ square units   _____ square units   _____ square units

6.   6 ft

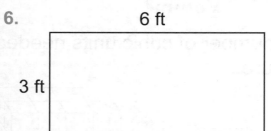

3 ft

7.   4m

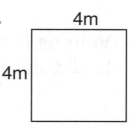

4m

8.

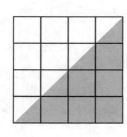

_____ square feet   _____ square mm   _____ square units

Place a dot at the coordinates of each ordered pair.
Connect the dots and find the area of each of the figures.

9. (2,2) (2,7) (8,2) (8,7)

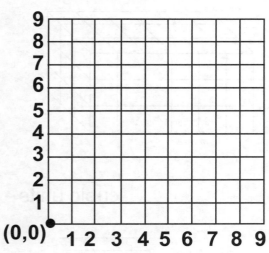

_____ square units

10. (6,6) (6,8) (8,6) (8,8)

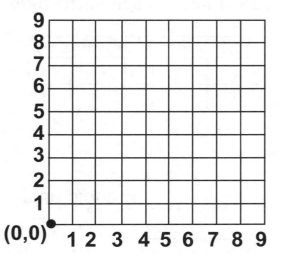

_____ square units

11. (2,2) (8,8) (8,2)

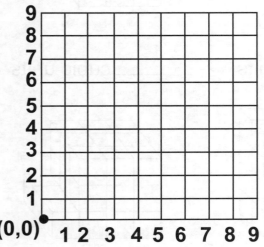

_____ square units

12. (1,2) (5,6) (5,2) (9,6)

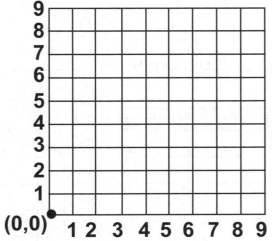

_____ square units

Area

169

Volume is the number of cubic units needed to fill a solid figure.

1 cubic unit

4 cubic units

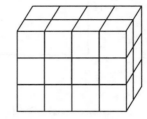
24 cubic units

Exercise

Find the volume of each of the figures.

1.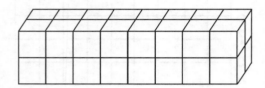

_____ cubic units

2.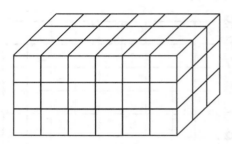

_____ cubic units

3.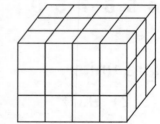

_____ cubic units

4.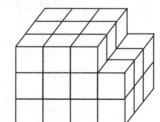

_____ cubic units

5.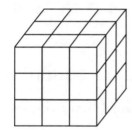

_____ cubic units

6.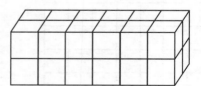

_____ cubic units

7.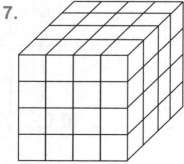

_____ cubic units

8.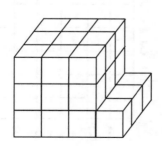

_____ cubic units

Volume

170

Exercise

Write the name of each figure.

1.

2.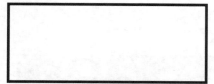

3.

_____   _____   _____

4.

5.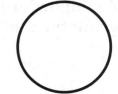

6.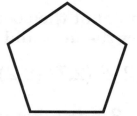

_____   _____   _____

Write the name of the triangles according to their sides.

7.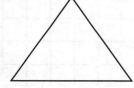

8.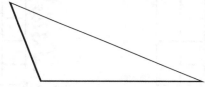

9.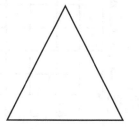

_____   _____   _____

Write the name of each triangle according to its angles.

10.

11.

12.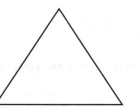

_____   _____   _____

13. Are these figures congruent?   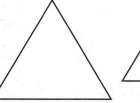   _____

14. Are they similar?   _____

15. Which is longer, a meter or a yard? _____

16. About how many centimeters are in an inch? _____

Measure with an inch ruler?

17. _____ in.

Measure with a centimeter ruler?

18. _____ cm

Place a dot at the coordinates of each ordered pair.
Connect the dots and find the perimeter and area of each of the figures.

19. (2,2) (2,7) (8,2) (8,7)

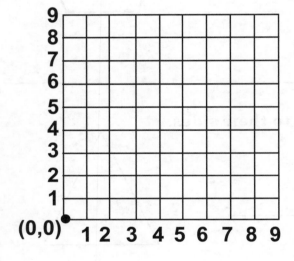

perimeter = _____ units

area = _____ square units

20. (6,6) (6,8) (8,6) (8,8)

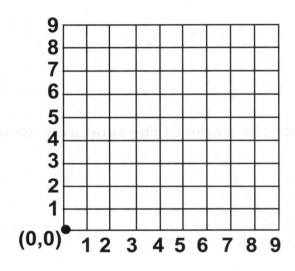

perimeter = _____ units

area = _____ square units

Find the volume of the figures.

21.

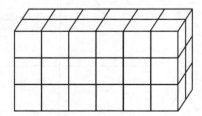

_____ cubic units

22.

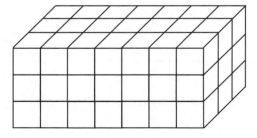

_____ cubic units

Maintaining Skills

Find the products.

1. 489
   × 5

2. 742
   × 6

3. 297
   × 2

4. 349
   × 3

5. 438
   × 6

6. 287
   × 4

7. 250
   × 3

8. 263
   × 8

9. $ 1.75
   × 8

10. $ 5.99
    × 4

11. $ 7.05
    × 5

12. $ 6.22
    × 8

Divide. Follow the steps. Use $ signs and decimals when necessary.

13. 5)425

14. 4)152

15. 7)546

16. 6)510

17. 7)333

18. 6)540

19. 8)493

20. 9)501

21. 4)$3.48

22. 4)$2.52

23. 3)$2.52

24. 8)$4.32

An **average** (also called the **mean**) is a quotient found by dividing the sum of a group of addends by the number of addends.

Example:

Find the average of the following numbers.

3, 5, 6, 2

First, we add up the numbers.

Then we take the sum and divide by the number of addends.

$$
\begin{array}{r}
3 \\
5 \\
6 \\
+\ 2 \\
\hline
16
\end{array}
\qquad
\begin{array}{r}
4 \\
4)\overline{16} \\
-16 \\
\hline
0
\end{array}
$$

The average of the numbers is 4.

Exercise

Find the average of each set of numbers.

1. 7, 12, 8

2. 6, 8, 12, 10

3. 3, 3, 9, 5, 8, 8,

———

———

———

4. 7, 8, 9

5. 8, 6, 4, 10, 7

6. 83, 93, 78, 96, 100

———

———

———

7. 3, 4, 5

8. 68, 72, 23, 15, 22

9. 30, 34, 31, 23, 27

———

———

———

Statistics – Average

10. 57, 46, 47   **11.** 59, 87, 63, 76, 60

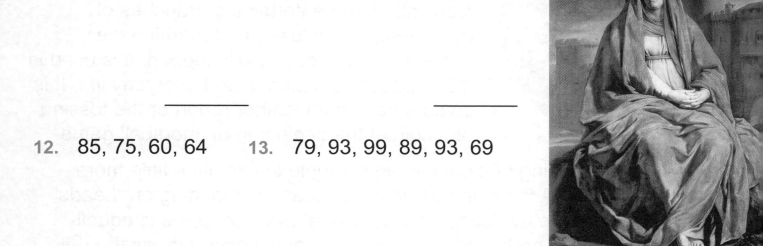

_____   _____

12. 85, 75, 60, 64   **13.** 79, 93, 99, 89, 93, 69

_____   _____

14. The four DeSoto children are ages 5, 8, 11, and 16.
What is the average age of the DeSoto children?

_____

15. The Knights of Columbus held a charity golf tournament.
On Friday, the winning score was 78, on Saturday,
it was 72, and on Sunday it was also 72.
What was the average winning score?

_____

16. The triangle has sides measuring 55cm, 50cm, and 42cm.
What is the average length of the sides of the triangle?

_____

17. John caught 6 fish, James caught 7 fish,
Peter caught 8 fish, Andrew caught 10 fish,
and Nathaniel caught 4 fish. What is the average
number of fish they caught.

_____

18. These are Sarah's quiz scores for last week: 75, 85, 96, 100
What was her average score?

_____

The theory of **probability** is one of the most fascinating and entertaining branches of mathematics. It is used to determine the chance that something will happen. It is used in many phases of science and everyday life. It is as common as a weather report or the tossing of a coin at the beginning of a football game.

Let's take the tossing of a coin as an example to explain a little more about probability. A fair coin has an equal chance of landing on "heads" or "tails." There are two possible **outcomes**. Each outcome is equally likely. We express probability of a particular event occurring as the ratio between the number of ways the particular event can happen and the total number of possible ways the equally likely events can happen. With a coin, the total number of ways that can happen are 2 and the way a particular thing (heads) is 1 so that the ratio of the coin turning up "heads" is 1 out of 2. We can write this as a fraction: $\frac{1}{2}$

What is the probability of a coin turning up "tails"?

How many ways are there for the coin to turn up "tails"?   1

How many possible ways are there for the coin to turn up?   2

The probability of a coin turning up "tails" is $\frac{1}{2}$.

As an experiment, take a coin and toss it 10 times and record your results. Then try it 100 times and write down the results.

A *die* is a cube with a number of dots on each of the six faces. Usually, the dots number from 1 to 6. In that case what is the probability that a 4 will turn up? Ask yourself:

How many ways can a 4 turn up?   1

How many possible ways are there for the die to turn up?   6

The probability of a die turning up 4 is $\frac{1}{6}$.

The spinner at the right is divided into four equal sections.

There are four possible outcomes. There is one 3.

The probability that the arrow will land on 3 is 1 out of 4.

The probability that the arrow will land on 3 is $\frac{1}{4}$.

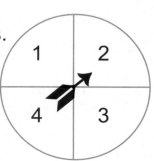

Probability

The spinner at the right is divided into six equal sections. There are six possible outcomes. Is there a 10? There is no 10 so the pointer cannot land on 10. It is an **impossible** event and the probability is **0**. Will the pointer land on a number less than 7? All the numbers are less than 7 and the event is **certain** and the probability is **1**.

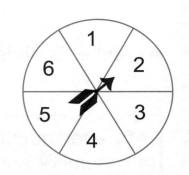

Exercise

Use the spinner at the right to answer the questions.

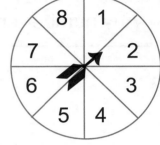

1.   What are the possible outcomes? _____

2.   How many different outcomes are possible? _____

3.   What is the probability of the pointer landing on 6? _____

Write the probability of the pointer landing on each number shown below.

4.   8 _____   5.   10 _____   6. 1 or 2 _____

Use the spinner at the right to answer the questions.

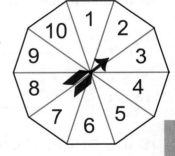

7.   What are the possible outcomes? _____

8.   How many different outcomes are possible? _____

9.   What is the probability of spinning a 6? _____

10.   What is the probability of spinning an even number? _____

11.   What is the probability of spinning a two digit number? _____

12.   What is the probability of spinning a 6, 7, or 8? _____

13.   What is the probability of spinning a 1? _____

14.   What is the probability of spinning a 0? _____

Divisibility

A number is **divisible** by another number when there is no remainder.

$$20 \div 2 = 10 \qquad 20 \div 5 = 4 \qquad 20 \div 10 = 2$$

Any even number is divisible by 2.
(any number ending in 0,2,4,6, or 8)

Any number ending in 0 or 5 is divisible by 5.

Any number ending in 0 is divisible by 10.

If the digits in a number add up to 9 or a number divisible by 9 then the number is divisible by 9.

Is the number divisible by 2? Write *Yes* or *No* and then tell why.

1. 24 _____

2. 30 _____

3. 278 _____

4. 343 _____

5. 4,127 _____

6. 3,332 _____

Is the number divisible by 5? Write *Yes* or *No* and then tell why.

7. 43 _____

8. 65 _____

9. 3,370 _____

10. 343 _____

11. 100 _____

12. 37 _____

Is the number divisible by 10? Write *Yes* or *No* and then tell why.

13. 340 _____

14. 100 _____

15. 305 _____

16. 750 _____

17. 635 _____

18. 99 _____

Is the number divisible by 9? Write *Yes* or *No* and then tell why.

19. 81 _____

20. 27 _____

21. 45 _____

22. 342 _____

23. 630 _____

24. 3744 _____

Order of Operations

When a problem has more than one operation, solve using the order of operations.

> ### Order of Operations
>
> *First* multiply or divide from left to right.
>
> *Then* add or subtract in order from left to right.

Solve $16 ÷ 8 + 3$

$16 ÷ 8 + 3$ Do the division first.

$2 + 3$ Then do the addition.

5

Study the examples.

$7 + 6 × 6 - 5$	$6 × 8 + 3 - 2$	Multiplication and division first.
$7 + 36 - 5$	$48 + 3 - 2$	Then addition and subtraction
$43 - 5$	$51 - 2$	from left to right.
38	49	

Exercise

Solve using the order of operations.

1. $36 - 15 ÷ 5$

    _____

2. $63 - 2 + 5$

    _____

3. $53 - 4 × 2$

    _____

4. $15 ÷ 5 × 2$

    _____

5. $5 × 3 + 7$

    _____

6. $6 + 8 × 2$

    _____

7. $6 + 6 ÷ 2$

    _____

8. $12 ÷ 3 + 4$

    _____

9. $48 - 36 ÷ 4$

    _____

Exercise

Solve using the order of operations.

1. $12 + 2 - 3 + 1$

2. $8 - 4 + 3 \times 5$

3. $40 \div 4 + 6 - 2$

4. $36 \div 9 - 3 + 6$

5. $10 - 3 + 2$

6. $3 + 2 \times 8 + 1$

7. $5 \times 8 + 9 \times 5$

8. $7 - 2 \times 3 + 1$

9. $9 \times 4 - 2 \times 6$

10. $48 \div 6 + 2$

11. $8 + 8 \div 4$

12. $70 - 63 \div 9$

13. $25 - 20 \div 5$

14. $16 \div 2 \times 12$

15. $8 \times 10 \div 2$

16. $7 + 6 \times 6 - 5$

17. $6 \times 8 + 3 - 2$

18. $28 \div 4 + 6 - 2$

19. $7 + 18 \div 3 + 2$

20. $4 + 10 - 3 \times 3$

21. $9 - 2 + 8 \div 4$

Missing Operation

When a problem is missing some pieces, it's like a puzzle. You have to try to figure out what it is that is missing. You try different pieces until you find one that fits. Here is a puzzle that is missing an operation. Do you remember the four operations? $(+ - \times \div)$

$8\bigcirc 4 = 32$ Can you think of a piece that would fit.

$8\left(+\right) 4 = 32$ Does this piece fit? $8 + 4 = 32$
No, because $8 + 4 = 12$. What will fit?

$8\left(\times\right) 4 = 32$ Does this piece fit? $8 \times 4 = 32$
Yes, because $8 \times 4 = 32$. The puzzle is solved.

Exercise

Solve by writing the correct operation.

1. $9\bigcirc 9 = 18$ 2. $7\bigcirc 7 = 0$ 3. $8\bigcirc 4 = 32$

4. $36\bigcirc 4 = 9$ 5. $8\bigcirc 6 = 48$ 6. $5\bigcirc 5 = 1$

7. $7\bigcirc 6 = 42$ 8. $6\bigcirc 4 = 24$ 9. $36\bigcirc 6 = 6$

10. $21\bigcirc 1 = 21$ 11. $8\bigcirc 8 = 1$ 12. $80\bigcirc 8 = 10$

13. $55\bigcirc 5 = 11$ 14. $3\bigcirc 10 = 30$ 15. $9\bigcirc 25 = 34$

16. $6\bigcirc 15 = 90$ 17. $80\bigcirc 8 = 88$ 18. $90\bigcirc 7 = 97$

19. $65\bigcirc 7 = 58$ 20. $54\bigcirc 6 = 9$ 21. $96\bigcirc 8 = 12$

22. $3\bigcirc 78 = 234$ 23. $23\bigcirc 3 = 20$ 24. $3\bigcirc 28 = 84$

25. $100\bigcirc 4 = 25$ 26. $9\bigcirc 6 = 15$ 27. $2\bigcirc 12 = 24$

Find the average of each set of numbers.

1. 7, 9, 8   2. 6, 4, 12, 10   3. 3, 7, 9, 5, 10, 8

_____   _____   _____

4. 16, 14, 9   5. 8, 6, 9, 10, 7   6. 86, 90, 78, 96, 100

_____   _____   _____

A cube with the letters **A**, **B**, **C**, **D**, **E**, and **F** is tossed.
Answer the following questions.

7. What are the possible outcomes? _____

8. How many different outcomes are possible? _____

9. What is the probability of tossing a B? _____

10. What is the probability of tossing a vowel? _____

11. What is the probability of tossing a consonant? _____

12. What is the probability of tossing a 7? _____

13. What is the probability of tossing a letter? _____

Is the number divisible by 2? Write *Yes* or *No.*

14. 35 _____   15. 30 _____   16. 152 _____

Is the number divisible by 5? Write *Yes* or *No.*

17. 152 _____   18. 30 _____   19. 275 _____

Is the number divisible by 10? Write *Yes* or *No.*

20. 240 _____   21. 508 _____   22. 275 _____

Is the number divisible by 9? Write *Yes* or *No.*

23. 36 _____   24. 81 _____   25. 378 _____

Solve using the order of operations.

26. $12 + 2 - 3 \times 1$ 27. $8 + 4 + 3 \times 5$ 28. $40 \div 10 + 6 - 2$

_____   _____   _____

29. $36 \div 4 - 3 + 6$ 30. $10 - 3 + 2$ 31. $3 + 2 \times 8 \times 1$

_____   _____   _____

32. $5 \times 8 + 9 \times 5$ 33. $7 - 2 \times 3 + 1$ 34. $9 \times 4 - 2 \times 6$

_____   _____   _____

Solve by writing the correct operation.

35. $9 \bigcirc 9 = 81$ 36. $7 \bigcirc 7 = 1$ 37. $8 \bigcirc 4 = 2$

38. $36 \bigcirc 4 = 32$ 39. $8 \bigcirc 6 = 48$ 40. $5 \bigcirc 5 = 0$

41. $7 \bigcirc 6 = 42$ 42. $6 \bigcirc 5 = 30$ 43. $36 \bigcirc 6 = 6$

Notes

Objective #1 – Addition and Subtraction Facts

The student will memorize the addition and subtraction facts through 18 and will demonstrate his mastery of the facts by completing Skill Tests for Objective #1 on pp. 187-189 quickly and accurately.

Objective #2 – Multiplication Facts

The student will memorize the multiplication facts through 81 and will demonstrate his mastery of the facts by completing the Skill Test for Objective #2 on pp. 190-191 quickly and accurately.

Objective #3 – Division Facts

The student will memorize the division facts through 81 and will demonstrate his mastery of the facts by completing the Skill Test for Objective #3 on pp. 192-193 quickly and accurately.

Objective #4 – Addition of Whole Numbers

The student will be able to add whole numbers and multiple addends up to the sum of 999,999 and will demonstrate his mastery by completing the Skill Test for Objective #4 on pp. 194-195 quickly and accurately.

Objective #5 – Subtraction of Whole Numbers

The student will be able to subtract up to 4-digit whole numbers and will demonstrate his mastery by completing the Skill Test for Objective #5 on pp. 196-197 quickly and accurately.

Notes

Objective #6 – Multiplication of Whole Numbers

The student will be able to multiply up to 3-digit whole numbers by 1-digit numbers and will demonstrate his mastery by completing the Skill Test for Objective #6 on pp. 198-199 quickly and accurately.

Objective #7 – Division of Whole Numbers

The student will be able to divide 2 and 3-digit dividends by 1-digit divisors resulting in 1, 2, or 3-digit quotients with and without remainders and will demonstrate his mastery by completing the Skill Test for Objective #7 on pp. 200-201 quickly and accurately.

Objective #8 – Fractions

The student will be able to find a fractional part of a number and be able to add and subract simple fractions with common denominators and will demonstrate his mastery by completing the Skill Test for Objective #8 on p. 202 quickly and accurately.

Objective #9 – Decimals and Fractions

The student will be able to write tenths and hundredths in both decimal and fraction form and be able to add and subract tenths and hundredths in decimal form and will demonstrate his mastery by completing the Skill Test for Objective #9 on p. 203 quickly and accurately.

Notes

You may make a copy of this page or write your answers on a different piece of paper, so that you may reuse this sheet, if necessary. You may also practice orally with your Mom or Dad or a brother or sister. **Remember: Speed and Accuracy.**

Find each sum.

1. $\begin{array}{r} 7 \\ + 9 \\ \hline \end{array}$ 2. $\begin{array}{r} 3 \\ + 9 \\ \hline \end{array}$ 3. $\begin{array}{r} 6 \\ + 9 \\ \hline \end{array}$ 4. $\begin{array}{r} 4 \\ + 8 \\ \hline \end{array}$ 5. $\begin{array}{r} 8 \\ + 9 \\ \hline \end{array}$ 6. $\begin{array}{r} 7 \\ + 8 \\ \hline \end{array}$

7. $\begin{array}{r} 8 \\ + 2 \\ \hline \end{array}$ 8. $\begin{array}{r} 4 \\ + 7 \\ \hline \end{array}$ 9. $\begin{array}{r} 4 \\ + 5 \\ \hline \end{array}$ 10. $\begin{array}{r} 6 \\ + 4 \\ \hline \end{array}$ 11. $\begin{array}{r} 5 \\ + 0 \\ \hline \end{array}$ 12. $\begin{array}{r} 3 \\ + 2 \\ \hline \end{array}$

13. $\begin{array}{r} 8 \\ + 8 \\ \hline \end{array}$ 14. $\begin{array}{r} 5 \\ + 7 \\ \hline \end{array}$ 15. $\begin{array}{r} 9 \\ + 5 \\ \hline \end{array}$ 16. $\begin{array}{r} 6 \\ + 6 \\ \hline \end{array}$ 17. $\begin{array}{r} 7 \\ + 7 \\ \hline \end{array}$ 18. $\begin{array}{r} 8 \\ + 7 \\ \hline \end{array}$

19. $\begin{array}{r} 9 \\ + 8 \\ \hline \end{array}$ 20. $\begin{array}{r} 7 \\ + 5 \\ \hline \end{array}$ 21. $\begin{array}{r} 2 \\ + 5 \\ \hline \end{array}$ 22. $\begin{array}{r} 5 \\ + 9 \\ \hline \end{array}$ 23. $\begin{array}{r} 8 \\ + 4 \\ \hline \end{array}$ 24. $\begin{array}{r} 6 \\ + 7 \\ \hline \end{array}$

25. $\begin{array}{r} 8 \\ + 3 \\ \hline \end{array}$ 26. $\begin{array}{r} 9 \\ + 7 \\ \hline \end{array}$ 27. $\begin{array}{r} 7 \\ + 7 \\ \hline \end{array}$ 28. $\begin{array}{r} 6 \\ + 8 \\ \hline \end{array}$ 29. $\begin{array}{r} 6 \\ + 6 \\ \hline \end{array}$ 30. $\begin{array}{r} 1 \\ + 1 \\ \hline \end{array}$

31. $\begin{array}{r} 5 \\ + 8 \\ \hline \end{array}$ 32. $\begin{array}{r} 9 \\ + 9 \\ \hline \end{array}$ 33. $\begin{array}{r} 8 \\ + 5 \\ \hline \end{array}$ 34. $\begin{array}{r} 7 \\ + 4 \\ \hline \end{array}$ 35. $\begin{array}{r} 5 \\ + 6 \\ \hline \end{array}$ 36. $\begin{array}{r} 8 \\ + 6 \\ \hline \end{array}$

37. $\begin{array}{r} 7 \\ + 6 \\ \hline \end{array}$ 38. $\begin{array}{r} 9 \\ + 4 \\ \hline \end{array}$ 39. $\begin{array}{r} 9 \\ + 6 \\ \hline \end{array}$ 40. $\begin{array}{r} 4 \\ + 3 \\ \hline \end{array}$ 41. $\begin{array}{r} 2 \\ + 4 \\ \hline \end{array}$ 42. $\begin{array}{r} 5 \\ + 5 \\ \hline \end{array}$

Speed _____   Accuracy _____ /42 = _____%

You may make a copy of this page or write your answers on a different piece of paper, so that you may reuse this sheet, if necessary. You may also practice orally with your Mom or Dad or a brother or sister. **Remember: Speed and Accuracy.**

Find each difference.

1. $\begin{array}{r} 4 \\ -2 \\ \hline \end{array}$
2. $\begin{array}{r} 12 \\ -5 \\ \hline \end{array}$
3. $\begin{array}{r} 9 \\ -1 \\ \hline \end{array}$
4. $\begin{array}{r} 8 \\ -5 \\ \hline \end{array}$
5. $\begin{array}{r} 12 \\ -9 \\ \hline \end{array}$
6. $\begin{array}{r} 16 \\ -7 \\ \hline \end{array}$

7. $\begin{array}{r} 6 \\ -0 \\ \hline \end{array}$
8. $\begin{array}{r} 11 \\ -5 \\ \hline \end{array}$
9. $\begin{array}{r} 10 \\ -3 \\ \hline \end{array}$
10. $\begin{array}{r} 11 \\ -6 \\ \hline \end{array}$
11. $\begin{array}{r} 5 \\ -4 \\ \hline \end{array}$
12. $\begin{array}{r} 10 \\ -9 \\ \hline \end{array}$

13. $\begin{array}{r} 11 \\ -2 \\ \hline \end{array}$
14. $\begin{array}{r} 10 \\ -7 \\ \hline \end{array}$
15. $\begin{array}{r} 14 \\ -5 \\ \hline \end{array}$
16. $\begin{array}{r} 13 \\ -7 \\ \hline \end{array}$
17. $\begin{array}{r} 6 \\ -3 \\ \hline \end{array}$
18. $\begin{array}{r} 15 \\ -6 \\ \hline \end{array}$

19. $\begin{array}{r} 17 \\ -9 \\ \hline \end{array}$
20. $\begin{array}{r} 10 \\ -4 \\ \hline \end{array}$
21. $\begin{array}{r} 14 \\ -9 \\ \hline \end{array}$
22. $\begin{array}{r} 13 \\ -5 \\ \hline \end{array}$
23. $\begin{array}{r} 15 \\ -8 \\ \hline \end{array}$
24. $\begin{array}{r} 17 \\ -9 \\ \hline \end{array}$

25. $\begin{array}{r} 10 \\ -6 \\ \hline \end{array}$
26. $\begin{array}{r} 6 \\ -2 \\ \hline \end{array}$
27. $\begin{array}{r} 17 \\ -8 \\ \hline \end{array}$
28. $\begin{array}{r} 8 \\ -8 \\ \hline \end{array}$
29. $\begin{array}{r} 11 \\ -7 \\ \hline \end{array}$
30. $\begin{array}{r} 9 \\ -6 \\ \hline \end{array}$

31. $\begin{array}{r} 12 \\ -6 \\ \hline \end{array}$
32. $\begin{array}{r} 13 \\ -6 \\ \hline \end{array}$
33. $\begin{array}{r} 12 \\ -7 \\ \hline \end{array}$
34. $\begin{array}{r} 10 \\ -2 \\ \hline \end{array}$
35. $\begin{array}{r} 12 \\ -3 \\ \hline \end{array}$
36. $\begin{array}{r} 13 \\ -9 \\ \hline \end{array}$

37. $\begin{array}{r} 11 \\ -3 \\ \hline \end{array}$
38. $\begin{array}{r} 18 \\ -9 \\ \hline \end{array}$
39. $\begin{array}{r} 16 \\ -8 \\ \hline \end{array}$
40. $\begin{array}{r} 14 \\ -7 \\ \hline \end{array}$
41. $\begin{array}{r} 15 \\ -9 \\ \hline \end{array}$
42. $\begin{array}{r} 9 \\ -2 \\ \hline \end{array}$

Speed _____ Accuracy _____ /42 = _____%

You may make a copy of this page or write your answers on a different piece of paper, so that you may reuse this sheet, if necessary. You may also practice orally with your Mom or Dad or a brother or sister. **Remember: Speed and Accuracy.**

Find each sum or difference. Watch the signs.

1. $\begin{array}{r} 16 \\ -\ 9 \\ \hline \end{array}$

2. $\begin{array}{r} 3 \\ +\ 2 \\ \hline \end{array}$

3. $\begin{array}{r} 6 \\ -\ 2 \\ \hline \end{array}$

4. $\begin{array}{r} 1 \\ +\ 6 \\ \hline \end{array}$

5. $\begin{array}{r} 8 \\ -\ 1 \\ \hline \end{array}$

6. $\begin{array}{r} 1 \\ +\ 1 \\ \hline \end{array}$

7. $\begin{array}{r} 7 \\ +\ 4 \\ \hline \end{array}$

8. $\begin{array}{r} 4 \\ -\ 1 \\ \hline \end{array}$

9. $\begin{array}{r} 6 \\ +\ 2 \\ \hline \end{array}$

10. $\begin{array}{r} 11 \\ -\ 4 \\ \hline \end{array}$

11. $\begin{array}{r} 7 \\ +\ 9 \\ \hline \end{array}$

12. $\begin{array}{r} 8 \\ -\ 6 \\ \hline \end{array}$

13. $\begin{array}{r} 15 \\ -\ 8 \\ \hline \end{array}$

14. $\begin{array}{r} 8 \\ +\ 4 \\ \hline \end{array}$

15. $\begin{array}{r} 9 \\ -\ 7 \\ \hline \end{array}$

16. $\begin{array}{r} 6 \\ +\ 9 \\ \hline \end{array}$

17. $\begin{array}{r} 13 \\ -\ 5 \\ \hline \end{array}$

18. $\begin{array}{r} 2 \\ +\ 3 \\ \hline \end{array}$

19. $\begin{array}{r} 7 \\ +\ 8 \\ \hline \end{array}$

20. $\begin{array}{r} 11 \\ -\ 6 \\ \hline \end{array}$

21. $\begin{array}{r} 8 \\ +\ 3 \\ \hline \end{array}$

22. $\begin{array}{r} 13 \\ -\ 4 \\ \hline \end{array}$

23. $\begin{array}{r} 4 \\ +\ 7 \\ \hline \end{array}$

24. $\begin{array}{r} 18 \\ -\ 9 \\ \hline \end{array}$

25. $\begin{array}{r} 11 \\ -\ 8 \\ \hline \end{array}$

26. $\begin{array}{r} 5 \\ +\ 4 \\ \hline \end{array}$

27. $\begin{array}{r} 13 \\ -\ 9 \\ \hline \end{array}$

28. $\begin{array}{r} 1 \\ +\ 7 \\ \hline \end{array}$

29. $\begin{array}{r} 16 \\ -\ 7 \\ \hline \end{array}$

30. $\begin{array}{r} 0 \\ +\ 0 \\ \hline \end{array}$

31. $\begin{array}{r} 9 \\ +\ 5 \\ \hline \end{array}$

32. $\begin{array}{r} 16 \\ -\ 8 \\ \hline \end{array}$

33. $\begin{array}{r} 7 \\ +\ 5 \\ \hline \end{array}$

34. $\begin{array}{r} 12 \\ -\ 5 \\ \hline \end{array}$

35. $\begin{array}{r} 6 \\ +\ 7 \\ \hline \end{array}$

36. $\begin{array}{r} 12 \\ -\ 6 \\ \hline \end{array}$

Speed _____   Accuracy _____ /36 = _____%

Congratulations!

You have completed your first objective! You may now put an X in the box next to it on page 185. Keep up the good work! God bless you!

You may make a copy of these pages or write your answers on a different piece of paper, so that you may reuse this drill, if necessary. You may also practice orally with your Mom or Dad or a brother or sister. **Remember: Speed and Accuracy.**

Multiply.

1. 9 × 9
2. 5 × 5
3. 4 × 6
4. 2 × 8
5. 8 × 9
6. 9 × 4

7. 7 × 5
8. 5 × 6
9. 6 × 8
10. 1 × 5
11. 9 × 2
12. 8 × 7

13. 7 × 6
14. 6 × 2
15. 5 × 9
16. 5 × 0
17. 2 × 4
18. 9 × 1

19. 8 × 2
20. 8 × 8
21. 8 × 5
22. 7 × 4
23. 5 × 8
24. 2 × 7

25. 3 × 3
26. 0 × 9
27. 9 × 6
28. 9 × 7
29. 7 × 8
30. 6 × 9

31. 5 × 4
32. 3 × 7
33. 4 × 5
34. 0 × 8
35. 6 × 6
36. 9 × 8

37. 6 × 4
38. 5 × 2
39. 3 × 9
40. 4 × 3
41. 4 × 9
42. 3 × 5

43. $\begin{array}{r} 0 \\ \times\,6 \\ \hline \end{array}$ 44. $\begin{array}{r} 1 \\ \times\,7 \\ \hline \end{array}$ 45. $\begin{array}{r} 2 \\ \times\,5 \\ \hline \end{array}$ 46. $\begin{array}{r} 3 \\ \times\,2 \\ \hline \end{array}$ 47. $\begin{array}{r} 5 \\ \times\,1 \\ \hline \end{array}$ 48. $\begin{array}{r} 6 \\ \times\,0 \\ \hline \end{array}$

49. $\begin{array}{r} 7 \\ \times\,1 \\ \hline \end{array}$ 50. $\begin{array}{r} 2 \\ \times\,2 \\ \hline \end{array}$ 51. $\begin{array}{r} 1 \\ \times\,4 \\ \hline \end{array}$ 52. $\begin{array}{r} 0 \\ \times\,5 \\ \hline \end{array}$ 53. $\begin{array}{r} 1 \\ \times\,9 \\ \hline \end{array}$ 54. $\begin{array}{r} 8 \\ \times\,1 \\ \hline \end{array}$

55. $0 \times 0 = $ _____   56. $2 \times 3 = $ _____   57. $3 \times 0 = $ _____

58. $2 \times 6 = $ _____   59. $3 \times 8 = $ _____   60. $5 \times 3 = $ _____

61. $7 \times 2 = $ _____   62. $8 \times 6 = $ _____   63. $4 \times 4 = $ _____

64. $0 \times 7 = $ _____   65. $3 \times 6 = $ _____   66. $4 \times 8 = $ _____

67. $5 \times 7 = $ _____   68. $2 \times 9 = $ _____   69. $8 \times 4 = $ _____

70. $6 \times 7 = $ _____   71. $8 \times 3 = $ _____   72. $3 \times 4 = $ _____

73. $6 \times 5 = $ _____   74. $7 \times 7 = $ _____   75. $9 \times 5 = $ _____

76. $6 \times 3 = $ _____   77. $7 \times 9 = $ _____   78. $9 \times 3 = $ _____

Speed _____   Accuracy _____ /78 = _____%

Congratulations!

You have completed your second objective! You may now put an X in the box next to it on page 185. Keep up the good work! God bless you!

You may make a copy of these pages or write your answers on a different piece of paper, so that you may reuse this drill, if necessary. You may also practice orally with your Mom or Dad or a brother or sister. **Remember: Speed and Accuracy.**

Divide.

1. 18 ÷ 2 = _____

2. 7)‾21‾

3. 20 ÷ 4 = _____

4. 2)‾10‾

5. 63 ÷ 9 = _____

6. 8)‾56‾

7. 64 ÷ 8 = _____

8. 9)‾9‾

9. 5 ÷ 5 = _____

10. 1)‾0‾

11. 0 ÷ 3 = _____

12. 2)‾6‾

13. 32 ÷ 8 = _____

14. 2)‾0‾

15. 1 ÷ 1 = _____

16. 8)‾24‾

17. 12 ÷ 2 = _____

18. 9)‾81‾

19. 42 ÷ 6 = _____

20. 9)‾27‾

21. 3 ÷ 1 = _____

22. 7)‾14‾

23. 6 ÷ 3 = _____

24. 8)‾0‾

25. 54 ÷ 9 = _____

26. 1)‾9‾

27. 18 ÷ 6 = _____

28. 7)‾7‾

29. 0 ÷ 4 = _____

30. 4)‾12‾

31. 30 ÷ 5 = _____

32. 5)‾30‾

33. 0 ÷ 1 = _____

34. 7)‾42‾

35. 12 ÷ 6 = _____

36. 1)‾2‾

37. 18 ÷ 3 = _____

38. 7)‾49‾

39. 72 ÷ 9 = _____

40. 3)‾27‾

41. 15 ÷ 5 = _____

42. 8)‾24‾

43. 36 ÷ 6 = _____

44. 9)‾27‾

45. $6 \div 2 =$ _____   46. $1\overline{)7}$ 47. $36 \div 9 =$ _____   48. $9\overline{)0}$

49. $63 \div 7 =$ _____   50. $7\overline{)56}$ 51. $72 \div 8 =$ _____   52. $5\overline{)45}$

53. $16 \div 4 =$ _____   54. $9\overline{)36}$ 55. $40 \div 5 =$ _____   56. $4\overline{)28}$

57. $0 \div 2 =$ _____   58. $5\overline{)20}$ 59. $9 \div 3 =$ _____   60. $8\overline{)48}$

61. $35 \div 5 =$ _____   62. $2\overline{)8}$ 63. $18 \div 9 =$ _____   64. $4\overline{)0}$

65. $21 \div 3 =$ _____   66. $4\overline{)32}$ 67. $28 \div 7 =$ _____   68. $5\overline{)10}$

69. $8 \div 1 =$ _____   70. $3\overline{)15}$ 71. $36 \div 4 =$ _____   72. $7\overline{)14}$

73. $4 \div 4 =$ _____   74. $5\overline{)25}$ 75. $12 \div 3 =$ _____   76. $3\overline{)24}$

77. $35 \div 7 =$ _____   78. $1\overline{)6}$ 79. $24 \div 6 =$ _____   80. $6\overline{)0}$

81. $0 \div 5 =$ _____   82. $6\overline{)6}$ 83. $16 \div 2 =$ _____   84. $1\overline{)4}$

Speed _____   Accuracy _____ /84 = _____%

Congratulations!

You have completed your third objective! You may now put an X in the box next to it on page 185. Keep up the good work! God bless you!

You may make a copy of these pages or write your answers on a different piece of paper, so that you may reuse this drill, if necessary. You may also practice orally with your Mom or Dad or a brother or sister. **Remember: Speed and Accuracy.**

Add.

1.
$$436$$
$$+ 527$$

2.
$$592$$
$$+ 408$$

3.
$$963$$
$$+ 79$$

4.
$$1800$$
$$+7470$$

5.
$$463$$
$$+ 364$$

6.
$$286$$
$$+ 414$$

7.
$$7096$$
$$+3142$$

8.
$$2754$$
$$+3943$$

9.
$$725$$
$$554$$
$$277$$
$$+ 342$$

10.
$$361$$
$$493$$
$$147$$
$$+ 229$$

11.
$$5922$$
$$6781$$
$$1831$$
$$+3001$$

12.
$$4850$$
$$5821$$
$$2132$$
$$+1976$$

13.
$$506$$
$$+ 434$$

14.
$$137$$
$$+ 548$$

15.
$$5462$$
$$+2915$$

16.
$$2234$$
$$+6952$$

17.
$$584$$
$$+ 643$$

18.
$$796$$
$$+ 254$$

19.
$$1748$$
$$+7797$$

20.
$$1969$$
$$+4238$$

21.
$$821$$
$$673$$
$$235$$
$$+ 111$$

22.
$$685$$
$$824$$
$$128$$
$$+ 467$$

23.
$$2925$$
$$1678$$
$$1183$$
$$+1300$$

24.
$$4568$$
$$8921$$
$$5831$$
$$+1308$$

25.
```
   485
 + 346
```

26.
```
   754
 + 196
```

27.
```
  3678
 +5145
```

28.
```
  3786
 +4283
```

29.
```
   128
   376
   532
 + 111
```

30.
```
   586
   428
   821
 + 764
```

31.
```
  2875
  6781
  5896
 +6434
```

32.
```
  8654
  1298
  1385
 +1830
```

33.
```
   324
 + 472
```

34.
```
   589
 + 723
```

35.
```
  1242
 +1596
```

36.
```
  3428
 +3178
```

37.
```
   487
 + 706
```

38.
```
   196
 + 754
```

39.
```
  1624
 +7967
```

40.
```
  5879
 +4283
```

41.
```
   312
   581
   497
 + 184
```

42.
```
   506
   625
   327
 + 517
```

43.
```
  2295
  1876
  1381
 +1003
```

44.
```
  3152
  1298
  1385
 +1830
```

Speed _____   Accuracy _____ /44 = _____%

Congratulations!

You have completed your fourth objective! You may now put an X in the box next to it on page 185. Keep up the good work! God bless you!

You may make a copy of these pages or write your answers on a different piece of paper, so that you may reuse this drill, if necessary. You may also practice orally with your Mom or Dad or a brother or sister. **Remember: Speed and Accuracy.**

Subtract.

1. $\begin{array}{r} 67 \\ -\ 48 \\ \hline \end{array}$
2. $\begin{array}{r} 50 \\ -\ 36 \\ \hline \end{array}$
3. $\begin{array}{r} 8316 \\ -\ 5597 \\ \hline \end{array}$
4. $\begin{array}{r} 5631 \\ -\ 2776 \\ \hline \end{array}$

5. $\begin{array}{r} 413 \\ -\ 242 \\ \hline \end{array}$
6. $\begin{array}{r} 531 \\ -\ 450 \\ \hline \end{array}$
7. $\begin{array}{r} 736 \\ -\ 643 \\ \hline \end{array}$
8. $\begin{array}{r} 345 \\ -\ 137 \\ \hline \end{array}$

9. $\begin{array}{r} 512 \\ -\ 234 \\ \hline \end{array}$
10. $\begin{array}{r} 650 \\ -\ 552 \\ \hline \end{array}$
11. $\begin{array}{r} 300 \\ -\ 256 \\ \hline \end{array}$
12. $\begin{array}{r} 580 \\ -\ 169 \\ \hline \end{array}$

13. $\begin{array}{r} 5432 \\ -\ 1189 \\ \hline \end{array}$
14. $\begin{array}{r} 7726 \\ -\ 5958 \\ \hline \end{array}$
15. $\begin{array}{r} 8512 \\ -\ 4888 \\ \hline \end{array}$
16. $\begin{array}{r} 4256 \\ -\ 1797 \\ \hline \end{array}$

17. $\begin{array}{r} 71 \\ -\ 63 \\ \hline \end{array}$
18. $\begin{array}{r} 63 \\ -\ 42 \\ \hline \end{array}$
19. $\begin{array}{r} 8243 \\ -\ 2658 \\ \hline \end{array}$
20. $\begin{array}{r} 6772 \\ -\ 4597 \\ \hline \end{array}$

21. $\begin{array}{r} 400 \\ -\ 274 \\ \hline \end{array}$
22. $\begin{array}{r} 504 \\ -\ 132 \\ \hline \end{array}$
23. $\begin{array}{r} 710 \\ -\ 368 \\ \hline \end{array}$
24. $\begin{array}{r} 800 \\ -\ 743 \\ \hline \end{array}$

25. 300
   − 245

26. 529
   − 471

27. 915
   − 256

28. 828
   − 575

29. 6600
   − 1981

30. 8416
   − 5859

31. 9524
   − 4888

32. 3475
   − 1797

33. 50
   − 31

34. 43
   − 36

35. 9056
   − 2776

36. 5631
   − 5597

37. 600
   − 265

38. 448
   − 276

39. 700
   − 299

40. 510
   − 286

41. 654
   − 149

42. 318
   − 257

43. 506
   − 256

44. 945
   − 169

45. 3574
   − 1189

46. 8614
   − 4888

47. 9425
   − 5958

48. 6006
   − 1797

Speed _____   Accuracy _____ /48 = _____%

Congratulations!

You have completed your fifth objective! You may now put an X in the box next to it on page 185. Keep up the good work! God bless you!

Skill Test for Objective #6 Multiplication

You may make a copy of these pages or write your answers on a different piece of paper, so that you may reuse this drill, if necessary. You may also practice orally with your Mom or Dad or a brother or sister. **Remember: Speed and Accuracy.**

Multiply.

1. 136 × 5

2. 356 × 7

3. 456 × 2

4. 234 × 3

5. 567 × 6

6. 124 × 4

7. 248 × 3

8. 653 × 8

9. 115 × 9

10. 847 × 6

11. 443 × 5

12. 765 × 4

13. 568 × 7

14. 690 × 8

15. 611 × 3

16. 271 × 4

17. 674 × 3

18. 793 × 2

19. 368 × 5

20. 484 × 7

21. 375 × 8

22. 216 × 3

23. 850 × 4

24. 781 × 6

25. 460 × 4

26. 329 × 5

27. 198 × 6

28. 748 × 9

29.   439
    ×   4

30.   689
    ×   3

31.   851
    ×   8

32.   575
    ×   7

33.   499
    ×   5

34.   712
    ×   6

35.   197
    ×   2

36.   149
    ×   3

37.   138
    ×   6

38.   278
    ×   4

39.   250
    ×   3

40.   273
    ×   8

41.   327
    ×   9

42.   297
    ×   6

43.   115
    ×   2

44.   957
    ×   6

45.   121
    ×   4

46.   127
    ×   8

47.   358
    ×   3

48.   341
    ×   4

49.   769
    ×   5

50.   532
    ×   7

51.   477
    ×   2

52.   265
    ×   3

Speed _____   Accuracy _____ /52 = _____%

Congratulations!

You have completed your sixth objective! You may now put an X in the box next to it on page 186. Keep up the good work! God bless you!

You may make a copy of these pages or write your answers on a different piece of paper, so that you may reuse this drill, if necessary. You may also practice orally with your Mom or Dad or a brother or sister. **Remember: Speed and Accuracy.**

Divide.

1. $3\overline{)31}$

2. $4\overline{)83}$

3. $2\overline{)61}$

4. $3\overline{)122}$

5. $4\overline{)243}$

6. $5\overline{)404}$

7. $6\overline{)365}$

8. $6\overline{)305}$

9. $8\overline{)407}$

10. $7\overline{)315}$

11. $9\overline{)824}$

12. $8\overline{)540}$

13. $8\overline{)614}$

14. $6\overline{)375}$

15. $6\overline{)243}$

16. $7\overline{)422}$

17. $5\overline{)434}$

18. $4\overline{)318}$

19. $9\overline{)673}$

20. $7\overline{)547}$

21. 3)91   22. 4)79   23. 7)90   24. 6)83

25. 8)768   26. 6)372   27. 5)245   28. 7)567

29. 3)297   30. 9)789   31. 6)528   32. 7)589

33. 8)387   34. 5)492   35. 4)397   36. 9)599

Speed _____ Accuracy _____ /36 = _____%

Congratulations!

You have completed your seventh objective! You may now put an X in the box next to it on page 186. Keep up the good work! God bless you!

You may make a copy of this page or write your answers on a different piece of paper, so that you may reuse this drill, if necessary. You may also practice orally with your Mom or Dad or a brother or sister. **Remember: Speed and Accuracy.**

Find the fraction of a number.

1. $\frac{1}{3}$ of 15 = _____

2. $\frac{1}{6}$ of 24 = _____

3. $\frac{4}{9}$ of 45 = _____

4. $\frac{3}{8}$ of 32 = _____

Find the sum.

5. $\frac{2}{4} + \frac{1}{4}$ = _____

6. $\frac{1}{2} + \frac{1}{2}$ = _____

7. $\frac{2}{6} + \frac{3}{6}$ = _____

8. $\frac{4}{10} + \frac{3}{10}$ = _____

9. $\frac{6}{12} + \frac{5}{12}$ = _____

10. $\frac{1}{15} + \frac{6}{15}$ = _____

Find the difference.

11. $\frac{4}{5} - \frac{2}{5}$ = _____

12. $\frac{3}{4} - \frac{1}{4}$ = _____

13. $\frac{4}{6} - \frac{3}{6}$ = _____

14. $\frac{6}{7} - \frac{2}{7}$ = _____

15. $\frac{5}{8} - \frac{3}{8}$ = _____

16. $\frac{9}{10} - \frac{6}{10}$ = _____

Congratulations!

You have completed your eighth objective! You may now put an X in the box next to it on page 186. Keep up the good work! God bless you!

You may make a copy of this page or write your answers on a different piece of paper, so that you may reuse this drill, if necessary. You may also practice orally with your Mom or Dad or a brother or sister. **Remember: Speed and Accuracy.**

Write each fraction as a decimal.

1. $\dfrac{3}{10}$ _____

2. $\dfrac{1}{100}$ _____

3. $\dfrac{23}{100}$ _____

Write each decimal as a fraction.

4. 0.3 _____

5. 0.35 _____

6. 0.07 _____

Add.

7.
$$\begin{array}{r} 2.4 \\ + 1.6 \\ \hline \end{array}$$

8.
$$\begin{array}{r} 3.9 \\ + 1.7 \\ \hline \end{array}$$

9.
$$\begin{array}{r} 7.4 \\ + 1.3 \\ \hline \end{array}$$

10.
$$\begin{array}{r} 5.9 \\ + 4.7 \\ \hline \end{array}$$

11.
$$\begin{array}{r} 30.21 \\ + 12.63 \\ \hline \end{array}$$

12.
$$\begin{array}{r} 34.78 \\ + 51.26 \\ \hline \end{array}$$

13.
$$\begin{array}{r} 0.79 \\ + 0.43 \\ \hline \end{array}$$

14.
$$\begin{array}{r} 6.5 \\ + 3.5 \\ \hline \end{array}$$

Subtract.

15.
$$\begin{array}{r} 9.52 \\ - 5.41 \\ \hline \end{array}$$

16.
$$\begin{array}{r} 2.39 \\ - 1.78 \\ \hline \end{array}$$

17.
$$\begin{array}{r} 7.48 \\ - 2.63 \\ \hline \end{array}$$

18.
$$\begin{array}{r} 8.26 \\ - 3.94 \\ \hline \end{array}$$

19.
$$\begin{array}{r} 0.7 \\ - 0.3 \\ \hline \end{array}$$

20.
$$\begin{array}{r} 7.00 \\ - 2.99 \\ \hline \end{array}$$

22.
$$\begin{array}{r} 1.5 \\ - 0.8 \\ \hline \end{array}$$

23.
$$\begin{array}{r} 8.0 \\ - 4.3 \\ \hline \end{array}$$

Congratulations!

You have completed your ninth objective! You may now put an X in the box next to it on page 186. Keep up the good work! God bless you!

Answer Key
Mathematics 3 for Young Catholics

p. 1

3	2	3	2
3	2	5	
3	2	5	
5			

1. 9   2. 9   3. 5   4. 10
5. 8   6. 8   7. 4   8. 10
9. 4   10. 10   11. 6   12. 2   13. 6   14. 0
15. 8   16. 5   17. 9   18. 10   19. 9   20. 6

p. 2

1. 2   2. 7   3. 9
4. 3   5. 9   6. 10
7. 10   8. 6   9. 0
10. 6   11. 8   12. 7
13. 5   14. 10   15. 6   16. 7   17. 7   18. 5
19. 3   20. 9   21. 4   22. 4   23. 9   24. 8
25. 3   26. 10   27. 7   28. 8   29. 9   30. 7
31. 8   32. 8   33. 10   34. 10   35. 4   36. 0
37. 9 pennies   38. 9 prayers

p. 3

8	7	8	7
8	7	15	
8	7	15	
15			

1. 14   2. 17   3. 11   4. 16
5. 12   6. 13   7. 12   8. 15
9. 13   10. 11   11. 15   12. 18   13. 12   14. 15
15. 12   16. 13   17. 11   18. 14   19. 11   20. 16

p. 4

1. 13   2. 12   3. 14
4. 14   5. 13   6. 13
7. 11   8. 15   9. 10
10. 18   11. 16   12. 10
13. 11   14. 11   15. 16   16. 11   17. 16   18. 14
19. 14   20. 12   21. 12   22. 13   23. 12   24. 12
25. 15   26. 14   27. 18   28. 13   29. 11   30. 17
31. 14   32. 11   33. 15   34. 16   35. 13   36. 14
37. 12 books   38. 16 runs

p. 5

10	4	4	10
10	4	6	
10	4	6	
6			

1. 6   2. 2   3. 7   4. 2
5. 4   6. 7   7. 2   8. 2
9. 5   10. 3   11. 5   12. 1   13. 4   14. 1
15. 5   16. 2   17. 4   18. 5   19. 1   20. 3

p. 6

1. 0   2. 4   3. 1
4. 0   5. 4   6. 6
7. 3   8. 1   9. 3
10. 5   11. 0   12. 3
13. 4   14. 2   15. 5   16. 1   17. 1   18. 3
19. 8   20. 5   21. 4   22. 0   23. 2   24. 1
25. 9   26. 6   27. 7   28. 0   29. 2   30. 0
31. 3   32. 7   33. 9   34. 2   35. 1   36. 2
37. 6 books   38. 5 points

p. 7

14	9	9	14
14	9	5	
14	9	5	
5			

1. 9   2. 6   3. 9   4. 4
5. 9   6. 8   7. 8   8. 7
9. 9   10. 6   11. 8   12. 5   13. 2   14. 9
15. 6   16. 9   17. 5   18. 7   19. 9   20. 6

p. 8

1. 8   2. 8   3. 7
4. 7   5. 7   6. 6
7. 4   8. 2   9. 7
10. 8   11. 9   12. 8
13. 8   14. 7   15. 6   16. 5   17. 8   18. 4
19. 9   20. 5   21. 7   22. 6   23. 6   24. 7
25. 9   26. 4   27. 8   28. 9   29. 12   30. 8
31. 2   32. 5   33. 8   34. 7   35. 7   36. 7
37. 9 chapters   38. 8 laps

p. 10

1. 12 12   2. 15 15
3. 12 12   4. 13 13   5. 14 14
6. 13 13   7. 17 17
8. 8 15 11 15   9. 8 14 9 14   10. 9 12 10 12

p. 11

1. No.   4-1=3 1-4≠3 Accept any reasonable example.
2. No.   (3-2)-1=0 3-(2-1)=2 Accept any reasonable example.
3. 8 8 8 8   4. 8 8
5. 15 8 15 8   6. 6 13 6 13
7. commutative   8. associative
9. identity   10. inverse operation

p. 12

1. subtraction   2. addition
3. subtracting   4. adding
5. 11 11 4   6. 13 13 8 5
7. 13 13 7 6   8. 13 13 4 9
9. 8 8 14   10. 5 5 7 12

11. 7 7 9 16   12. 4 4 5 9
13. 7   14. 6   15. 5   16. 4   17. 3   18. 9
19. 14   20. 10   21. 13   22. 13   23. 10   24. 14

p. 13-14

1. 4 horses   2. 8 children   3. 8 cars
4. 9 girls   5. 17 points   6. 9 hours
7. 10 chapters   8. 8 chapters
9. 7 chapters   10. 13 chapters
11. 5 chapters   12. 15 chapters
13. 8 chapters

p. 15

1. 9 9   2. 8 8   3. 10 10
4. 16 16   5. 15 15   6. 12 12
7. 6, 9, 12, 15, 18, 21, 24, 27
8. 10, 15, 20, 25, 30, 35, 40, 45
9. 4, 6, 8, 10, 12, 14, 16, 18
10. 8, 12, 16, 20, 24, 28, 32, 36

p. 16

0	0	0	0	0	0
0	1	2	3	4	5
0	2	4	6	8	10
0	3	6	9	12	15
0	4	8	12	16	20
0	5	10	15	20	25

1. 12 12   2. 10 10
3. 8 8   4. 5 5   5. 0 0

p. 17

0	0	0	0	0	0	0	0	0	0
0	1	2	3	4	5	6	7	8	9
0	2	4	6	8	10	12	14	16	18
0	3	6	9	12	15	18	21	24	27
0	4	8	12	16	20	24	28	32	36
0	5	10	15	20	25	30	35	40	45
0	6	12	18	24	30	36	42	48	54
0	7	14	21	28	35	42	49	56	63
0	8	16	24	32	40	48	56	64	72
0	9	18	27	36	45	54	63	72	81

10 10 100

p. 18

0	0	0	0	0	0	0	0	0	0
0	1	2	3	4	5	6	7	8	9
0	2	4	6	8	10	12	14	16	18
0	3	6	9	12	15	18	21	24	27
0	4	8	12	16	20	24	28	32	36
0	5	10	15	20	25	30	35	40	45
0	6	12	18	24	30	36	42	48	54
0	7	14	21	28	35	42	49	56	63
0	8	16	24	32	40	48	56	64	72
0	9	18	27	36	45	54	63	72	81

p. 19

1. 6   2. 9   3. 0   4. 0
5. 3   6. 0   7. 4   8. 12
9. 8   10. 8   11. 9   12. 0   13. 10   14. 0

9	12	15	18	21	24	27
12	16	20	24	28	32	36
15	20	25	30	35	40	45
18	24	30	36	42	48	54
21	28	35	42	49	56	63
24	32	40	48	56	64	72
27	36	45	54	63	72	81

p. 21

1. 6, 9, 12, 15, 18, 21, 24, 27
2. 8, 12, 16, 20, 24, 28, 32, 36
3. 10, 15, 20, 25, 30, 35, 40, 45
4. 9   5. 12   6. 15   7. 18
8. 12   9. 16   10. 20   11. 24
12. 15   13. 20   14. 25   15. 30
16. 21   17. 24   18. 27   19. 28   20. 32   21. 36
22. 35   23. 40   24. 45   25. 6   26. 8   27. 10
28. 0   29. 8   30. 18   31. 0   32. 8   33. 14

p. 22

0	0	0
3	4	5
6	8	10
9	12	15
12	16	20
15	20	25
18	24	30
21	28	35
24	32	40
27	36	45

1. 18   2. 24   3. 21
4. 36   5. 24   6. 32
7. 35   8. 40   9. 45

p. 23

1. 12, 18, 24, 30, 36, 42, 48, 54
2. 14, 21, 28, 35, 42, 49, 56, 63
3. 35   4. 36   5. 42   6. 48
7. 54   8. 42   9. 49   10. 56
11. 63   12. 24   13. 30   14. 28
15. 35   16. 18   17. 42   18. 48   19. 63   20. 28

0	3	6	9	12	15	18	21	24	27
0	4	8	12	16	20	24	28	32	36
0	5	10	15	20	25	30	35	40	45
0	6	12	18	24	30	36	42	48	54
0	7	14	21	28	35	42	49	56	63

p. 24

0	0
6	7
12	14

18	21
24	28
30	35
36	42
42	49
48	56
54	63

1. 18 2. 21
3. 28 4. 24
5. 30 6. 35
7. 6 8. 18 9. 30 10. 42 11. 54 12. 0
13. 12 14. 24 15. 36 16. 49 17. 35 18. 21
19. 7 20. 63 21. 56 22. 42 23. 28 24. 14

p. 25

1. 16, 24, 32, 40, 48, 56, 64, 72
2. 18, 27, 36, 45, 54, 63, 72, 81
3. 48 4. 56 5. 64 6. 72
7. 54 8. 63 9. 72 10. 81
11. 32 12. 40 13. 36 14. 45
15. 24 16. 56 17. 64 18. 81 19. 36 20. 45

	0	5	10	15	20	25	30	35	40	45
	0	6	12	18	24	30	36	42	48	54
	0	7	14	21	28	35	42	49	56	63
	0	8	16	24	32	40	48	56	64	72
	0	9	18	27	36	45	54	63	72	81

p. 26

0	0
8	9
16	18
24	27
32	36
40	45
48	54
56	63
64	72
72	81

1. 24 2. 27
3. 36 4. 32
5. 40 6. 45
7. 8 8. 24 9. 40 10. 56 11. 72 12. 0
13. 16 14. 32 15. 48 16. 63 17. 45 18. 27
19. 9 20. 81 21. 72 22. 54 23. 36 24. 18

p. 27

1. 18 2. 18 3. 56 4. 56
5. 30 6. 30 7. 21 8. 21
9. 32 10. 32 11. 42 12. 42
13. 27 14. 27 15. 40 16. 40
17. 100 18. 121 19. 144
20. 99 21. 110 22. 120
23. 90 24. 88 25. 77
26. 5 27. 3 28. 6 29. 8 30. 4
31. 0 32. 0 33. 0 34. 0 35. 0

p. 28-29

1. 27 minutes 2. 24 chocolates 3. 28 plants
4. 16 hours 5. 18 points 6. 40 pennies
7. 12 fish 8. 72 candles 9. 18 runs
10. 21 chapters 11. 30 desks 12. 36 problems
13. 49 marbles 14. 15 hours 15. 64 squares

p. 30

1. 15 2. 9 3. 15 4. 14 5. 9 6. 10
7. 7 laps
8. 7 9. 9 10. 6 11. 8 12. 5 13. 4
14. 6 tomato plants
15. 0 16. 6 17. 0
18. 14 19. 48 20. 16
21. 21
22. 9 23. 0 24. 0 25. 25 26. 6 27. 36
28. 64 29. 20 30. 42 31. 81 32. 49 33. 72

p. 31

1. 12÷3=4   12÷4=3
2. 20÷4=5   20÷5=4
3. 21÷3=7   21÷7=3
4. 16÷2=8   16÷8=2

p. 32

4 4
1. 4 2. 3 3. 3 4. 4
5. 3 6. 3 7. 3 8. 4

p. 33

1. 3 3 9 ÷ 3 = 3
2. 4 4 16 ÷ 4 = 4
3. 5 5 25 ÷ 5 = 5

p. 34

1. 6 6 36 ÷ 6 = 6
2. 7 7 49 ÷ 7 = 7
3. 8 8 64 ÷ 8 = 8
4. 9 9 81 ÷ 9 = 9
5. 1 6. 15 7. 0
8. 10 9. 0 10. 1
11. 0 12. 1 13. 21

p. 35

1. 9 2. 7
3. 5 4. 8
5. 4 6. 3
7. 2 8. 6
9. 1 10. 1
11. 0 12. 7
13. 9 22. 9 31. 9
14. 8 23. 8 32. 8
15. 7 24. 7 33. 7
16. 6 25. 6 34. 6
17. 5 26. 5 35. 5
18. 4 27. 4 36. 4
19. 3 28. 3 37. 3
20. 2 29. 2 38. 2
21. 1 30. 1 39. 1

Answer Key

p. 36

1. 9			2. 4		
3. 8			4. 5		
5. 4			6. 9		
7. 4			8. 7		
9. 5			10. 7		
11. 6			12. 7		
13. 9		22. 9		31. 9	
14. 8		23. 8		32. 8	
15. 7		24. 7		33. 7	
16. 6		25. 6		34. 6	
17. 5		26. 5		35. 5	
18. 4		27. 4		36. 4	
19. 3		28. 3		37. 3	
20. 2		29. 2		38. 2	
21. 1		30. 1		39. 1	

p. 37

1. 9	2. 8	3. 7
4. 6	5. 5	6. 4
7. 3	8. 2	9. 1
10. 9	11. 8	12. 7
13. 6	14. 5	15. 4
16. 3	17. 2	18. 1
19. 7	20. 9	21. 9
22. 4	23. 7	24. 6
25. 3	26. 8	27. 6
28. 3	29. 8	30. 8
31. 4	32. 8	33. 9
34. 6	35. 3	36. 5

p. 38

1. 8	2. 8	3. 3	4. 3
5. 4	6. 4	7. 3	8. 3
9. 2	10. 2	11. 9	12. 9
13. 9	14. 9	15. 2	16. 2
17. 5	18. 7	19. 8	20. 9
21. 5	22. 5	23. 4	24. 7
25. 5	26. 6	27. 9	28. 5
29. 8	30. 7		

p. 39

1. 1	2. 2	3. 7	
4. 1	5. 2	6. 2	
7. 3	8. 4	9. 9	
10. 4	11. 8	12. 4	13. 2
14. 2	15. 8	16. 3	17. 3
18. 4	19. 6	20. 7	
21. 3	22. 5	23. 9	
24. 4	25. 8	26. 7	
27. 5	28. 6	29. 5	
30. 9	31. 9	32. 7	
33. 16	34. 8	35. 4	

p. 42

1. 59	2. 90
3. 37	4. 84
5. 15	6. 42
7. 63	8. 36
9. 71	10. 28
11. 7 9	12. 5 5
13. 2 6	14. 3 2
15. 5 8	16. 8 3
17. 6 4	18. 9 1

p. 43

1. 123	2. 518
3. 345	4. 836
5. 567	6. 954
7. 789	8. 672
9. 200	10. 491

p. 44-45

1. 713	2. 985
3. 372	4. 528
5. 231	6. 864
7. 159	8. 447

9. 3 6 2 300 60 2
10. 5 9 1 500 90 1
11. 7 4 3 700 40 3
12. 5 6 8 500 60 8
13. 4 5 3 400 50 3
14. 9 8 1 900 80 1
15. 6 7 4 600 70 4
16. 8 6 5 800 60 5

p. 45

1. 15	2. 14	3. 15	4. 14	5. 9	6. 10
7. 7	8. 6	9. 6	10. 9	11. 5	12. 4
13. 9	14. 0	15. 21	16. 25	17. 12	18. 36
19. 6	20. 8	21. 5	22. 3		
23. 3	24. 4	25. 4	26. 3		
27. 3	28. 2	29. 8	30. 9		

p. 46

1. 8162	2. 2811
3. 6384	4. 9639
5. 4546	6. 7450
7. 2728	8. 5277
9. 1903	10. 3095

p. 47

1. 5323	2. 2525
3. 9747	4. 6968
5. 3286	6. 8474
7. 7692	

p. 48

1. 76,381	2. 59,563
3. 94,745	4. 27,927
5. 43,292	6. 88,474
7. 65,656	8. 32,838

p. 49

1. 31,421	2. 64,535
3. 27,619	4. 52,446
5. 70,259	6. 45,726

p. 50-51

1. 3 6 9 4 5 0
2. 1 2 3 4 5 6
3. 6 8 7 2 9 1
4. 3 3 5 9 5 1
5. 7 1 7 2 4 1
6. 2 4 9 3 0 9
7. 5 2 5 7 5 0
8. 4 7 5 3 0 0
9. 5 9 6 0 1 5

p. 52-53

1. 749,635 700,000 40,000 9,000 600 30 5
2. 881,242 800,000 80,000 1,000 200 40 2
3. 953,719 900,000 50,000 3,000 700 10 9
4. 609,866 600,000 9,000 800 60 6
5. 715,259 700,000 10,000 5,000 200 50 9
6. 145,356 100,000 40,000 5,000 300 50 6
7. 412,776 400,000 10,000 2,000 700 70 6
8. 557,275 500,000 50,000 7,000 200 70 5
9. 241,907 200,000 40,000 1,000 900 7

p. 54

1. 2479
2. 6917
3. 8778
4. 3254
5. 123
6. 7987
7. 4312
8. 7000
9. 5613
10. 5943
11. 7296
12. 3215

p. 55

1. 3492
2. 798
3. 4385
4. 928
5. 7789
6. 2295
7. 8576
8. 9663
9. 3523
10. 6847
11. 6840
12. 37,465
13. 5987
14. 92,987

p. 56

1. <
2. >
3. >
4. <
5. <
6. >
7. <
8. <
9. <
10. >
11. >
12. <
13. >
14. <
15. <
16. <
17. <
18. >
19. >
20. <
21. <
22. <

p. 57

50   60   60
1. 30
2. 70
3. 100
4. 370
5. 50
6. 120
7. 200
8. 340

p. 58

1. 70
2. 2490
3. 1250
4. 100
5. 150
6. 490

7. 30
8. 630
9. 40
10. 48,240
11. 440
12. 90
13. 30
14. 12,820

p. 59

1. 200
2. 700
3. 6900
4. 900
5. 2900
6. 900
7. 300
8. 2400
9. 500
10. 9900
11. 700
12. 900
13. 900
14. 8,000

p. 60

1. 6000
2. 4,000
3. 62,000
4. 9,000
5. 44,000
6. 8,000
7. 93,000
8. 66,000
9. 82,000
10. 76,000
11. 54,000
12. 87,000

p. 61

1. 67,020
2. 430
3. 380
4. 5,490
5. 8920
6. 560
7. 780
8. 54,930
9. 2700
10. 200
11. 400
12. 500
13. 2500
14. 3600
15. 900
16. 900
17. 4000
18. 91,000
19. 46,000
20. 8,000
21. 7000
22. 68,000
23. 79,000
24. 55,000

p. 62

1. 629,455 600,000 20,000 9,000 400 50 5
2. 473,639 400,000 70,000 3,000 600 30 9
3. 593,215 500,000 90,000 3,000 200 10 5
4. <
5. <
6. <
7. <
8. <
9. >
10. >
11. >
12. >
13. <

p. 63

1. 72 2. 96 3. 59 4. 68 5. 92
6. 72 7. 69 8. 99 9. 48 10. 81
11. 77 12. 76 13. 79 14. 89 15. 94
16. 79 plants   17. 48 children

p. 64

5866

p. 65

1. 86 2. 85 3. 99 4. 76 5. 98
6. 987 7. 698 8. 999 9. 598
10. 888   11. 8694   12. 7958

13. 7888   14. 7798   15. 7796
16. 7997   17. 6884   18. 6791
19. 5,689 new students   20. 517 miles

p. 66

1. 62   2. 85   3. 80   4. 64   5. 72
6. 85 hot dogs

p. 67

1. 91   2. 57   3. 75   4. 72   5. 90
6. 98   7. 81   8. 84   9. 63   10. 84
11. 73   12. 72   13. 94
14. 97   15. 63   16. 92
17. 46   18. 62   19. 56
20. 141 acres   21. 62 points

p. 68

1. 627   2. 857   3. 805
4. 646   5. 698   6. 914

p. 69

1. 7385   2. 5288   3. 7567   4. 9176
5. 9297   6. 7366   7. 8684   8. 8136
9. 9172   10. 7546   11. 7068   12. 8878

p. 71

1. 136   2. 149   3. 109   4. 162
5. 123   6. 962   7. 823   8. 634
9. 810   10. 942   11. 751
12. 4372   13. 7531   14. 8212
15. 9425   16. 9730   17. 8285
18. 114 minutes   19. 6754 paces

p. 72

1. 924 potatoes   2. 625 miles
3. 900 points   4. 919 jelly beans
5. 9,109 pounds   6. 6,315 km
7. 8,533 labels   8. 5,813 apples

p. 74

1. 959   2. 902   3. 1789   4. 1872
5. 14,292   6. 19,446   7. 11,129
8. 6129   9. 8159   10. 12,470
11. 16,118 12. 8794 13. 17,890 14. 5870
15. 263,262

p. 75

1. $10.21 2. $4.62 3. $9.66 4. $8.00
5. $7.94 6. $8.04 7. $8.42 8. $7.47
9. $9.78 10. $27.08

p. 76

1. $16.51 2. $9.87 3. $14.07 4. $13.34
5. $9.61 6. $5.41 7. $10.01 8. $9.95
9. $8.30 10. $10.18 11. $11.33 12. $6.33
13. $14.04 14. $8.05 15. $10.17 16. $9.20
17. $14.20 18. $8.54
19. $16.89 20. $17.48

p. 77

1. 64   2. 91   3. 80   4. 95
5. 85   6. 824   7. 704   8. 701
9. 311   10. 761   11. 9217   12. 6024
13. 831   14. 950   15. 9544   16. 6279
17. 1147   18. 2599   19. 6555   20. 13,167
21. $11.62 22. $14.76 23. $10.55 24. $9.44
25. $9.09 26. $9.22 27. $8.71 28. $9.00

p. 78

1. 924 peanuts   2. 625 apples
3. 900 altogether   4. 919 miles
5. 18,218 vegetables   6. 15,424 altogether
7. $14.11

p. 79

1. 314   2. 451   3. 166   4. 647
5. 725   6. 501   7. 152   8. 206
9. 613   10. 331   11. 102   12. 270
13. 241 pages

p. 80

3   13
6   15
8   14
6   2   14
5   12   14

p. 81

1. 484   2. 367   3. 681   4. 83
5. 349   6. 93   7. 534   8. 466

p. 82

1. 476   2. 358   3. 678   4. 79
5. 290   6. 498   7. 337   8. 368

p. 83

1. 79   2. 487   3. 266   4. 454
5. 85   6. 349   7. 285   8. 242
9. 116   10. 459   11. 578   12. 776
13. 256   14. 552   15. 517   16. 568
17. 277 strawberries   18. 167 miles
19. 74 contestants

p. 85

1. 34   2. 8   3. 269   4. 183
5. 2683   6. 1828   7. 1267   8. 2777
9. 767   10. 667   11. 1869   12. 1583
13. 828   14. 1778   15. 1977   16. 1369
17. 378 cattle   18. 1665 things   19. 76 more

p. 86

1. 17   2. 37   3. 5768   4. 7766
5. 249   6. 88   7. 5909   8. 2566
9. 5582   10. 5127   11. 5678   12. 875
13. 178 apples   14. 2777 widgets   15. 77 people
16. 167 marbles   17. 687 tickets

p. 87

1. $1.79 2. $4.80 3. $3.48 4. $2.74
5. $18.74 6. $47.35 7. $3.77 8. $24.78
9. $27.88

p. 88

1. $41.09 2. $24.90 3. $38.96 4. $27.58
5. $27.58 6. $25.02 7. $33.59 8. $27.61
9. $48.99 10. $28.38 11. $26.11 12. $10.89
13. $31.89 14. $18.89 15. $18.90 16. $11.99
17. $1.88 18. $1.50 19. $4.82 20. $68.81

p. 89

1. 25 2. 9 3. 3459 4. 2855
5. $24.12 6. $11.66 7. $45.85 8. $32.29
9. 3688 10. $16.65 11. 749 12. $7.44
13. 4817 14. 2656 15. 4537 16. 1777
17. 269 stamps 18. $3.87
19. 6075 miles 20. $2.05

p. 90

1. 5 2. 12 3. 15 4. 18 5. 9 6. 13
7. 4 8. 6 9. 3 10. 8 11. 5 12. 3
13. 54 14. 0 15. 28 16. 25 17. 18 18. 36
19. 63 20. 6 21. 20 22. 63 23. 32 24. 56
25. 12 26. 16 27. 45 28. 42 29. 14 30. 54
31. 6 32. 8 33. 5 34. 2 35. 3 36. 2
37. 4 38. 3 39. 3 40. 2 41. 8 42. 9

p. 91-92

1. 7 2. 49
   70 490
   700 4900
   7000 49,000
3. 4 4. 16
   40 160
   400 1600
   4000 16,000
5. 8 6. 64
   80 640
   800 6400
   8000 64,000
7. 2 8. 10
   20 100
   200 1000
   2000 10,000
9. 3 10. 18
   30 180
   300 1800
   3000 18,000

p. 93-94

1. 30 × 7 = 210   6 × 7 = 42   252
2. 200 × 4 = 800 ; 40 × 4 = 160 ; 3 × 4 = 12 ; 972
3. 20 × 6 = 120   7 × 6 = 42   162
4. 100 × 4 = 400 ; 80 × 4 = 320 ; 9 × 4 = 36 ; 756
5. 10 × 9 = 90   4 × 9 = 36   126
6. 40 × 8 = 320   2 × 8 = 16   336
7. 100 × 5 = 500 ; 40 × 5 = 200 ; 6 × 5 = 30 ; 730

p. 95

1. 555 2. 987 3. 848 4. 669
5. 682 6. 999 7. 862 8. 892
9. 286 10. 397 11. 696 12. 888

p. 97

1. 648 2. 542 3. 846 4. 924
5. 771 6. 1022 7. 788 8. 732
9. 566 10. 790 11. 740 12. 718
13. 1758 14. 834 15. 594 16. 1935

p. 98

1. 954 2. 860 3. 861 4. 704
5. 789 6. 685 7. 750 8. 612
9. 552 10. 916 11. 936 12. 715
13. 816 14. 3195 15. 2786 16. 852
17. 1736 18. 1112 19. 945 20. 1482
21. 714 peaches 22. 612 pages
23. 335 passengers

p. 99

1. $8.25 2. $7.78 3. $9.75 4. $6.76
5. $9.42 6. $7.44 7. $9.38 8. $7.74

p. 100

1. $8.10 2. $6.04 3. $5.12 4. $5.79
5. $8.00 6. $6.52 7. $7.41 8. $19.35
9. $41.13 10. $23.22 11. $19.24 12. $66.56
13. $16.73 14. $13.95 15. $50.61 16. $77.76
17. $9.92 18. $8.76 19. $8.96 20. $8.15

p. 101

1. 2495 2. 4272 3. 394 4. 447
5. 828 6. 1112 7. 750 8. 2184
9. 2943 10. 1782 11. 230 12. 5742
13. 1756 14. 5512 15. 2553 16. 2300
17. $13.68 18. $21.56 19. $35.25 20. $49.68
21. $5.52 22. $65.79 23. $13.23 24. $13.98
25. $53.76 26. $23.32 27. $16.45 28. $51.04
29. $54.00 30. $35.58 31. $31.32 32. $39.56

p. 102

1. 1935 plants 2. $22.85
3. 2322 nuts 4. $11.24
5. 6656 miles 6. $18.95
7. 2778 widgets 8. $18.20

p. 103

1. 5 2. 8 3. 4 4. 6
5. 9 6. 5 7. 8 8. 7
9. 6 10. 4 11. 5 12. 6
13. 7 14. 8 15. 4 16. 6
17. 8 18. 7 19. 3 20. 3
21. 8 22. 5 23. 8 24. 7
25. 7 26. 9 27. 9 28. 6
29. 5 30. 7 31. 5 32. 7
33. 2 34. 8 35. 3 36. 6
37. 3 38. 9 39. 4 40. 3
41. 7 42. 4 43. 4 44. 9

p. 104-105

1. 6 R 2
2. 6 R 1
3. 5 R 2
4. 3 R 4
5. 3 R 3
6. 6 R 3
7. 2 R 4
8. 5 R 5
9. 7 R 2
10. 5 R 5
11. 8 R 3
12. 8 R 1

p. 106

1. 6 R 2
2. 4 R 2
3. 3 R 2
4. 2 R 3
5. 9 R 2
6. 3 R 1
7. 6 R 2
8. 4 R 4
9. 29 R 1
10. 12 R 1
11. 17 R 2
12. 24 R 1
13. 24
14. 23
15. 15 R 2
16. 11
17. 13
18. 14
19. 13
20. 12 R 5

p. 107

1. 10 family members
2. 8 cans
3. 4 eggs
4. 6 games
5. 8 problems per day
6. 12 rows with 3 seeds left over
7. 21 cards on each wall
8. 11 stamps on each page with 6 left over
9. 20 quarts with 2 cups left over

p. 108

1. 24 R 1
2. 18
3. 17
4. 12 R 2
5. 17 R 1
6. 27 R 2
7. 24
8. 31
9. 11
10. 23
11. 8 R 6
12. 3 R 3

p. 109

1. 61
2. 62
3. 54 R 3
4. 35

p. 110

1. 66
2. 66
3. 50 R 2
4. 40 R 4
5. 40 R 5
6. 61
7. 72
8. 78 R 2
9. 94
10. 82
11. 62
12. 97
13. 32
14. 93
15. 91 R 1
16. 53 R 4
17. 39 R 2
18. 71
19. 55
20. 21

p. 111

1. $.38
2. $.38
3. $.31
4. $.43

p. 112

1. 13 R 3
2. 12 R 5
3. 16 R 1
4. 23 R 2
5. 10 R 1
6. 26 R 1
7. 12 R 6
8. 16 R 3
9. 83
10. 37
11. 77
12. 84
13. 63 R 3
14. 89
15. 61 R 4
16. 44 R 5
17. $.86
18. $.62
19. $.83
20. $.53

p. 113

1. 1/4
2. 3/4
3. 1/3
4. 2/3
5. 1/2
6. 1/2
7. 4/5

p. 114

1. 3/10
2. 1/3
3. 5/12
4. 9/16
5. 3/8
6. 3/5
7. 1/2
8. 3/4
9. 4/5
10. 2/5
11. 5/8
12. 5/10
13. 3/7

p. 115

1. 1/4
2. 1/3
3. 1/2
4. 3/10
5. 2/3
6. 1/6
7. 5/8
8. 2/7
9. 2/3
10. 3/4
11. 7/8
12. 1/5
13. 5/10
14. 1/12
15. 9/10
16. one fourth
17. three fourths
18. two fifths
19. four fifths
20. two thirds
21. one third
22. three fifths
23. one sixth
24. one eighth
25. one tenth

p. 116

Answers will vary. Examine drawings.

p. 117

Answers may vary

1. 2/4, 3/6, 4/8, 5/10, 6/12, 8/16
2. 2/8, 3/12, 4/16
3. 1/3, 2/6, 3/9
4. 3/4, 6/8, 9/12
5. 2/10,
6. 2/3, 6/9, 8/12
7. 3/4, 9/12, 12/16

p. 118

1. 3/6
2. 2/8
3. 8/12
4. 8/16
5. 5/15
6. 4/10
7. 4/12
8. 10/10

p. 121

1. 2/12
2. 6/10
3. 3/9
4. 1/4
5. 4/8
6. 6/12
7. 2/6
8. 2/8
9. 1/3
10. 4/10
11. 6/8
12. 2/4
13. 1/5
14. 4/5
15. 1/2
16. 9/12
17. 5/6
18. 3/5
19. 2/3
20. 1/2

p. 122

Answers will vary

p. 123

1. <
2. <
3. <
4. <
5. >
6. <
7. >
8. <
9. >
10. >
11. <
12. <
13. >
14. >
15. <
16. <
17. >
18. <
19. <
20. >
21. <

p. 124

1. >
2. =
3. <
4. >
5. >
6. <
7. >
8. >
9. <
10. >
11. =
12. <

p. 125

1. 4
2. 4
3. 5
4. 8
5. 9
6. 5
7. 5
8. 4
9. 5
10. 7
11. 3
12. 9
13. 3

p. 126

1. 6
2. 16
3. 15
4. 24

p. 127
1. 5 are boys
2. 3 are girls
3. 8 candles were lit
4. 19 cards
5. 12 jellybeans
6. 20 questions right
7. 40 points
8. 5 people
9. 24 students

p. 128
1. 2 1/4
2. 2 3/4
3. 2 1/8
4. 1 5/6
5. 2 1/2
6. 1 5/8
7. 1 4/5
8. 1 3/10
9. 3 1/2
10. 3 2/3

p. 129
1. 3/4
2. 7/9
3. 5/6
4. 8/8
5. 8/10
6. 6/12
7. 3/5

p. 130
1. 1/4
2. 2/9
3. 2/6
4. 3/8
5. 5/10
6. 7/12
7. 3/5

p. 131
1. 3/4
2. 3/3
3. 5/6
4. 5/10
5. 7/12
6. 5/15
7. 2/5
8. 5/6
9. 7/8
10. 4/7
11. 7/9
12. 3/5
13. 1/3
14. 2/4
15. 2/6
16. 2/7
17. 5/8
18. 1/10
19. 3/10
20. 3/8
21. 1/4
22. 2/8
23. 4/12
24. 2/5

p. 132
1. 3/5 of the field
2. 2/5 of the field
3. 2/7 of a week
4. 2/7 of a week
5. 4/8 of a mile
6. 3/6 of the pizza
7. 3/6 of the pizza
8. 6/12 of her time

p. 133
1. 4/12
2. 8/10
3–5. anwers will vary
6. >
7. <
8. <
9. =
10. <
11. >
12. 6
13. 7
14. 6
15. 8
16. 10
17. 9
18. 20
19. 2 3/8
20. 1 7/10

p. 134
1. 7
2. 5
3. 4
4. 7
5. 7
6. 2
7. 11
8. 3
9. 8
10. 7
11. 16
12. 2
13. 42
14. 12
15. 45
16. 0
17. 8
18. 9
19. 16
20. 64
21. 40
22. 28
23. 40
24. 14
25. 1840
26. 1645
27. 1188
28. 6732
29. 1147
30. 2599
31. 21,986
32. 13,167
33. 796
34. 1312
35. 2838
36. 6606

p. 135-136
1. 3/10   0.3   three tenths
2. 30/100   0.30   thirty hundredths
3. 7/10   0.7   seven tenths
4. 37/100   0.37   thirty-seven hundredths
5. 6/10   0.6   six tenths
6. 50/100   0.50   fifty hundredths
7. 9/10   0.9   nine tenths
8. 63/100   0.63   sixty-three hundredths
9. 4/10   0.4   four tenths
10. 75/100   0.75   seventy-five hundredths
11. 5/10   0.5   five tenths
12. 25/100   0.25   twenty-five hundredths

p. 137
1. 0.3
2. 0.7
3. 0.5
4. 0.01
5. 0.23
6. 0.59
7. 0.2
8. 0.8
9. 0.6
10. 0.04
11. 0.55
12. 0.99
13. 0.1
14. 0.5
15. 0.9
16. 0.07
17. 0.20
18. 0.14

p. 138
1. 3/10
2. 5/10
3. 7/10
4. 21/100
5. 35/100
6. 75/100
7. 4/10
8. 6/10
9. 8/10
10. 99/100
11. 1/100
12. 11/100
13. 3/10
14. 5/10
15. 7/10
16. 7/100
17. 20/100
18. 14/100

p. 139
1. 3.4
2. 5.8
3. 7.1
4. 21.34
5. 35.36
6. 75.28
7. 4.9
8. 6.7
9. 8.2
10. 99.92
11. 11.20
12. 15.90
13. 55.05
14. 9.7
15. 22.08
16. 80.01
17. 17.75
18. 15.3

p. 140
1. thee and seven tenths
2. twenty-one and nine tenths
3. four and twenty-three hundredths
4. nine and eight tenths
5. fifty and five tenths
6. seven and forty-four hundredths
7. seventy-five

p. 141
1. 4.79
2. 69.17
3. 9.98
4. 32.54
5. 1.23
6. 9.87
7. 3.1
8. 6.0
9. 3.59
10. 7.8
11. 96.2
12. 32.15

p. 142
1. 3.52
2. 0.29
3. 0.98
4. 1.54
5. 0.78
6. 0.87
7. 3.1
8. 3.60
9. 0.59
10. 4.8
11. 0.6
12. 0.29

p. 143
1. >
2. >
3. <
4. >
5. >
6. <
7. <
8. <
9. <

10.	<	11.	<	12.	>
13.	<	14.	>	15.	>
16.	>	17.	<	18.	<
19.	<	20.	>		

p. 144

1. 3.8	2. 6.2	3. 8.6	4. 11.1
5. 0.47	6. 1.79	7. 1.09	8. 10.0
9. 3.81	10. 8.02	11. 5.95	12. 64.51
13. 52.97	14. 86.39	15. 1.19	16. 2.3
17. 0.7	18. 1.0	19. 56.10	20. 35.95

p. 145

1. 5.09	2. 7.44	3. 6.21	4. 2.23
5. 0.3	6. 3.01	7. 0.7	8. 2.7
9. 1.50	10. 1.67	11. 2.58	12. 4.31
13. 1.8	14. 1.7	15. 0.4	16. 5.6

p. 146

1. 8.6	2. 6.6	3. 14.7	4. 10.0
5. 0.36	6. 0.62	7. 5.4	8. 11.1
9. 5.85	10. 7.30	11. 8.00	12. 10.00
13. 5.08	14. 3.1	15. 4.13	16. 3.64
17. 4.4	18. 2.56	19. 3.3	20. 5.1
21. 3.78	22. 6.4	23. 0.36	24. 3.36

p. 147

1. 1.6 miles	2. 2.25 miles
3. 21.8 lbs	4. 0.7
5. 0.3	6. 3.4
7. 1.6	8. Peter
9. 0.3 km	10. 0.35
11. $2.03	

p. 148

1. 0.5	2. 0.4	3. 0.1
4. 0.49	5. 0.04	6. 0.10
7. 0.3	8. 0.05	9. 0.30
10. 1/10	11. 6/10	12. 9/10
13. 25/100	14. 89/100	15. 1/100
16. 2.7	17. 3.9	18. 9.1
19. 33.07	20. 14.50	21. 97.35
22. >	23. <	24. < 25. >

p. 150

1. no	2. yes	3. yes	4. yes	5. no
6. no	7. yes	8. yes	9. no	

p. 151

1. line segment	2. none	3. line
4. line	5. ray	6. none
7. none	8. line segment	9. ray

p. 152

1. parallel	2. parallel
3. intersect	4. intersect
5. parallel	6. intersect
7. examine drawing	8. examine drawing

p. 153

1. right	2. obtuse	3. obtuse
4. acute	5. right	6. acute
7. examine drawing	8. examine drawing	

p. 154-155

1. 0	2. 1	3. 4
4. square	5. rectangle	
6. circle	7. triangle	
8. pentagon	9. hexagon	

10.–18. examine drawings

19. 4	20. 3	21. 4	22. 5	23. 4	24. 7
25. 80 R5	26. 31	27. 82	28. 58 R2		

p. 157

1. equilateral	2. scalene
3. isosceles	4. scalene
5. right	6. obtuse
7. acute	8. equilateral, equiangular
9. right, isosceles	10. obtuse, scalene

p. 159

1. trapezoid	2. parallelogram
3. rectangle	4. rhombus
5. square 6. yes	7. no 8. no
9. yes 10. yes	11-13. examine drawings

p. 160

1. first and fourth	2. second and third
3. third and fourth	4. second and fourth
5. first and third	6. third and fourth

p. 161

1. first and fourth	2. second and third
3. third and fourth	4. first and fourth
5. second and fourth	

p. 162

1. G	2. F	3. E	4. D	5. C	6. B
7. (4,3)		8. (2,6)		9. (3,8)	
10. (6,7)		11. (9,5)		12. (7,4)	

p. 163

1. G	2. F	3. E	4. D	5. C	6. B
7. J	8. H	9. A	10. I	11. L	12. K
13. (3,1)		14. (4,3)		15. (2,5)	
16. (4,7)		17. (5,8)		18. (8,7)	
19. (7,5)		20. (8,3)		21. (6,1)	
22. (1,8)		23. (7,9)			

p. 165

1. 12 in.	2. 3 ft	3. 2½cm
4. 39 in.	5. 5280 ft	6. 36 in.

p. 166

1. 5	2. 3	3. 4½	4. 3½	5. 2	6. 1
7. 13	8. 7	9. 9	10. 6	11. 8	12. 11

p. 167
1. 18 ft   2. 30 in.   3. 3 yd   4. 42 mm
5. 32 cm   6. 77 m   7. 60 in.

p. 168-169
1. 16   2. 16   3. 12   4. 18   5. 12   6. 18
7. 16   8. 8   9. 30   10. 4   11. 18   12. 16

p. 170
1. 32   2. 54   3. 36   4. 33
5. 27   6. 24   7. 64   8. 30

p. 171-172
1. square   2. rectangle   3. hexagon
4. triangle   5. circle   6. pentagon
7. equilateral   8. scalene   9. isosceles
10. right   11. obtuse   12. equilateral
13. no   14. yes   15. meter
16. 2½   17. 4 not exact in this edition.
18. 11 not exact in this edition.
19. 22 30   20. 8 4   21. 36
22. 63

p. 173
1. 2445   2. 4452   3. 594   4. 1047
5. 2628   6. 1148   7. 750   8. 2104
9. $14.00   10. $23.96   11. $35.25   12. $49.76
13. 85   14. 38   15. 78   16. 85
17. 47 R4   18. 90   19. 61 R5   20. 55 R6
21. $0.87   22. $0.63   23. $0.84   24. $0.54

p. 174-175
1. 9   2. 9   3. 6
4. 8   5. 7   6. 90
7. 4   8. 40   9. 29
10. 50   11. 69   12. 71
13. 87   14. 10   15. 74
16. 49   17. 7   18. 89

p. 177
1. 1-8   2. 8   3. 1/8   4. 1/8
5. 0   6. 2/8   7. 1-10   8. 10
9. 1/10   10. 5/10   11. 1/10   12. 3/10
13. 1/10   14. 0

p. 178
1. yes   2. yes   3. yes
4. no   5. no   6. yes
7. no   8. yes   9. yes
10. no   11. yes   12. no
13. yes   14. yes   15. no
16. yes   17. no   18. no
19. yes   20. yes   21. yes
22. yes   23. yes   24. yes

p. 179
1. 33   2. 66   3. 45
4. 6   5. 22   6. 22
7. 9   8. 8   9. 39

p. 180
1. 12   2. 19   3. 14
4. 7   5. 9   6. 20
7. 85   8. 2   9. 24
10. 10   11. 10   12. 63
13. 21   14. 96   15. 40
16. 38   17. 49   18. 11
19. 15   20. 5   21. 9

p. 181
1. +   2. −   3. ×
4. ÷   5. ×   6. ÷
7. ×   8. ×   9. ÷
10. ÷ or ×   11. ÷   12. ÷
13. ÷   14. ×   15. +
16. ×   17. +   18. +
19. −   20. ÷   21. ÷
22. ×   23. −   24. ×
25. ÷   26. +   27. ×

p. 182-183
1. 8   2. 8   3. 7   4. 13
5. 8   6. 90   7. ABCDEF   8. 6
9. 1/6   10. 2/6   11. 4/6   12. 0
13. 1   14. no   15. yes   16. yes
17. no   18. yes   19. yes   20. yes
21. no   22. no   23. yes   24. yes
25. yes   26. 11   27. 27   28. 8
29. 12   30. 9   31. 19   32. 85
33. 2   34. 24   35. ×   36. ÷
37. ÷   38. −   39. ×   40. −
41. ×   42. ×   43. ÷

Objectives Skills Tests

p. 187
1. 16   2. 12   3. 15   4. 12   5. 17   6. 15
7. 10   8. 11   9. 9   10. 10   11. 5   12. 5
13. 16   14. 12   15. 14   16. 12   17. 14   18. 15
19. 17   20. 12   21. 7   22. 14   23. 12   24. 13
25. 11   26. 16   27. 14   28. 14   29. 12   30. 2
31. 13   32. 18   33. 13   34. 11   35. 11   36. 14
37. 13   38. 13   39. 15   40. 7   41. 6   42. 10

p. 188
1. 2   2. 7   3. 8   4. 3   5. 3   6. 9
7. 6   8. 6   9. 7   10. 5   11. 1   12. 1
13. 9   14. 3   15. 9   16. 6   17. 3   18. 9
19. 8   20. 6   21. 5   22. 8   23. 7   24. 8
25. 4   26. 4   27. 9   28. 0   29. 4   30. 3
31. 6   32. 7   33. 5   34. 8   35. 9   36. 4
37. 8   38. 9   39. 8   40. 7   41. 6   42. 7

p. 189
1. 7   2. 5   3. 4   4. 7   5. 7   6. 2
7. 11   8. 3   9. 8   10. 7   11. 16   12. 2
13. 7   14. 12   15. 2   16. 15   17. 8   18. 5
19. 15   20. 5   21. 11   22. 9   23. 11   24. 9

25. 3   26. 9   27. 4   28. 8   29. 9   30. 0
31. 14   32. 8   33. 12   34. 7   35. 13   36. 6

p. 190-191

1. 81   2. 25   3. 24   4. 16   5. 72   6. 36
7. 35   8. 30   9. 48   10. 5   11. 18   12. 56
13. 42   14. 12   15. 45   16. 0   17. 8   18. 9
19. 16   20. 64   21. 40   22. 28   23. 40   24. 14
25. 9   26. 0   27. 54   28. 63   29. 56   30. 54
31. 20   32. 21   33. 20   34. 0   35. 36   36. 72
37. 24   38. 10   39. 27   40. 12   41. 36   42. 15
43. 0   44. 7   45. 10   46. 6   47. 5   48. 0
49. 7   50. 4   51. 4   52. 0   53. 9   54. 8
55. 0   56. 6   57. 0
58. 12   59. 24   60. 15
61. 14   62. 48   63. 16
64. 0   65. 18   66. 32
67. 35   68. 18   69. 32
70. 42   71. 24   72. 12
73. 30   74. 49   75. 45
76. 18   77. 63   78. 27

p. 192-193

1. 9   2. 3   3. 5   4. 5
5. 7   6. 7   7. 8   8. 1
9. 1   10. 0   11. 0   12. 3
13. 4   14. 0   15. 1   16. 3
17. 6   18. 9   19. 7   20. 3
21. 3   22. 2   23. 2   24. 0
25. 6   26. 9   27. 3   28. 1
29. 0   30. 3   31. 6   32. 6
33. 0   34. 6   35. 2   36. 2
37. 6   38. 7   39. 8   40. 9
41. 3   42. 3   43. 6   44. 3
45. 3   46. 7   47. 4   48. 0
49. 9   50. 8   51. 9   52. 9
53. 4   54. 4   55. 8   56. 7
57. 0   58. 4   59. 3   60. 6
61. 7   62. 4   63. 2   64. 0
65. 7   66. 8   67. 4   68. 2
69. 8   70. 5   71. 9   72. 2
73. 1   74. 5   75. 4   76. 8
77. 5   78. 6   79. 4   80. 0
81. 0   82. 1   83. 8   84. 4

p. 194-195

1. 963   2. 1000   3. 1042   4. 9270
5. 827   6. 700   7. 10,238   8. 6697
9. 1898   10. 1230   11. 17,535   12. 14,779
13. 940   14. 685   15. 8377   16. 9186
17. 1227   18. 1050   19. 9545   20. 6207
21. 1840   22. 2104   23. 7086   24. 20,628
25. 831   26. 950   27. 8823   28. 8069
29. 1147   30. 2599   31. 21,986   32. 13,167
33. 796   34. 1312   35. 2838   36. 6606
37. 1193   38. 950   39. 9591   40. 10,162
41. 1574   42. 1975   43. 6555   44. 7665

p. 196-197

1. 19   2. 14   3. 2719   4. 2855
5. 171   6. 81   7. 93   8. 208
9. 278   10. 98   11. 44   12. 411
13. 4243   14. 1768   15. 3624   16. 2459
17. 8   18. 21   19. 5585   20. 2175
21. 126   22. 372   23. 342   24. 57
25. 55   26. 58   27. 659   28. 253
29. 4619   30. 2557   31. 4636   32. 1678
33. 19   34. 7   35. 6280   36. 34
37. 335   38. 172   39. 401   40. 224
41. 505   42. 61   43. 250   44. 776
45. 2385   46. 3726   47. 3467   48. 4209

p. 198-199

1. 680   2. 2492   3. 912   4. 702
5. 3402   6. 496   7. 744   8. 5224
9. 1035   10. 5082   11. 2215   12. 3060
13. 3976   14. 5520   15. 1833   16. 1084
17. 2022   18. 1586   19. 1840   20. 3388
21. 3000   22. 648   23. 3400   24. 4686
25. 1840   26. 1645   27. 1188   28. 6732
29. 1756   30. 2067   31. 6808   32. 4025
33. 2495   34. 4272   35. 394   36. 447
37. 828   38. 1112   39. 750   40. 2184
41. 2943   42. 1782   43. 230   44. 5742
45. 484   46. 1016   47. 1074   48. 1364
49. 3845   50. 3724   51. 954   52. 795

p. 200-201

1. 10 R1   2. 20 R3   3. 30 R1   4. 40 R2
5. 60 R3   6. 80 R4   7. 60 R5   8. 50 R5
9. 50 R7   10. 45   11. 91 R5   12. 67 R4
13. 76 R6   14. 62 R3   15. 40 R3   16. 60 R2
17. 86 R4   18. 79 R2   19. 74 R7   20. 78 R1
21. 30 R1   22. 19 R3   23. 12 R6   24. 13 R5
25. 96   26. 62   27. 49   28. 81
29. 99   30. 87 R6   31. 88   32. 84 R1
33. 48 R3   34. 98 R2   35. 99 R1   36. 66 R5

p. 202

1. 5   2. 4   3. 20
4. 12   5. 3/4   6. 2/2
7. 5/6   8. 7/10   9. 11/12
10. 7/15   11. 2/5   12. 2/4
13. 1/6   14. 4/7   15. 2/8
16. 3/10

p. 203

1. 0.3   2. 0.01   3. 0.23
4. 3/10   5. 35/100   6. 7/100
7. 4.0   8. 5.6   9. 8.7
10. 10.6   11. 42.84   12. 86.04
13. 1.22   14. 10.0   15. 4.11
16. 0.61   17. 4.85   18. 4.32
19. 0.4   20. 4.01   21. 0.7
22. 3.7

Like our books?

You might like our program, too. Seton Home Study School offers a full curriculum program for Kindergarten through Twelfth Grade. We include daily lesson plans, answer keys, quarterly tests, and much more. Our staff of teachers and counselors is available to answer questions and offer help. We keep student records and send out diplomas that are backed by our accreditation with the Southern Association of Colleges and Schools and the Commission on International and Transregional Accreditation.

For more information about Seton Home Study School, please contact our admissions office.

Seton Home Study School
1350 Progress Drive
Front Royal, VA 22630

Phone: 540-636-9990 • Fax: 540-636-1602
Internet: www.setonhome.org • E-mail: info@setonhome.org